in your
UNDERWEAR

life in intentional christian community

edited by
BRIAN SANDERS

Published by Underground Media

www.undergroundglobal.org

© 2011 Underground Media

Cover Design by Jessie Rajski
Interior Design by Jon Dengler

For information or bulk orders:
UNDERGROUND MEDIA
1300 E 7TH AVE
TAMPA FL 33605
813.248.3301

Library of Congress Cataloging in Publication Data is available upon request.

ISBN 978-0-9845758-1-7

Printed in the United States

undergroundmedia

To The Underground:
A community for our community

Table of Contents:

Foreword

The best way to start a book like this is to simply tell our story. Not the whole story of course, and not our individual stories, but our collective story. We will start with our story together. In 1995, I (Brian) was hired by a para church campus ministry and placed in Tampa to pioneer work at the large local state university. I was 23, married to Monica and we had one luminous daughter, Jael. As the campus ministry was planted and grew, Monica and I also had a longing to work with and for the poor.

Urbana 96 solidified that call for me and I felt moved to find a home in the inner city where an intentional community could be formed to simply love our neighbors in a hurting neighborhood. I invited Jason and Katy to move to Tampa and help realize that vision. With the help of a generous friend I was able to borrow the money to buy two houses back to back. The students would eventually name this duplex the Tampa house and it started with the four of us. Within a few months the first student moved in.

After 2 years the house was full. Jessica was one of my first student leaders, faithful and dependable; she was one of the first students to move into the house. I soon paired her with another strong student leader named Jeremy to co-lead a bible study on campus. I thought they would make a good team. It seems they agreed and eventually married each other, but not before Jeremy moved in to the house, too. Crystal was also a faithful student leader and as soon as she graduated she accepted my invitation to try out life in the house with us. Jennifer was a student leader who ran out of money for housing so I offered her a place with us. We made the back house quarters for the single guys and the women lived in the front house with the two married couples. But we shared one kitchen and ate all our meals together. We were committed to four things (this was our covenant with each other): Jesus and the nurture of our personal relationship with him; community and the care and attention to invest in our relationships with each other; campus, having all agreed that our ministry was not to the inner city, but to the campus, our common mission field; and the neighborhood, even though it was not our primary calling we committed that we would not be missionary tourists in the neighborhood. If we were going to be there we wanted to serve the neighborhood and make it better in some small way because of our presence.

The campus ministry grew and we started a year round tutoring program in the neighborhood. We partnered with a local elementary school and a summer urban project that was open to college students from all around the country. It quickly became clear that we were going to be a bridge between the need of the neighborhood and the resources of the university. But I think the partnership worked so well because we discovered along the way that in this beautiful exchange, we were needed too and there were resources in the neighborhood that were drawing us all closer to Jesus.

In 1999, I became the area director for that campus ministry. Jason was hired, and soon Jessica, and then Jeremy. Jeremy and Jessica married and pioneered a campus ministry at the local community college. It was a remarkable ministry in itself, and Joann was one of the first students they met on campus. She became a leader in their ministry and I eventually hired her to be my assistant. In 2000, we were able to buy a bigger house about a mile from the Tampa house. It came with a mother in law suite in the back and we were able to convert the house to have 8 bedrooms. Joann eventually moved in to the house in 2003. Jeremy and Jessica lived in that house until 2004, when after the birth of their second child they bought a small 2 bedroom house a few blocks away. Every Sunday night, for all these years we have gathered in our living room to laugh, pray, listen, and share our burdens and joys with each other.

Jennifer finished nursing school and became a hospice nurse. Katy worked as a pediatric nurse. Crystal has worked steadily as an actor and teacher. Joann stayed my assistant until 2005. Jason did campus ministry on one campus while Jeremy and Jessica worked on another. I became the director of the ministry for the state of Florida and although we were living together in many ways I felt like we were fragmented, and I longed for the days when we were all doing the same ministry. That, coupled with our collective frustration about traditional church (see my other book *Life After Church*), moved us to start a house church. Being able to do ministry together again was invigorating for us. And because we lived in a needy neighborhood there was no shortage of adventure in our weekly meetings.

Still I felt restless, like we were supposed to do more. We started a small network of house churches (about 5) and we began praying and meeting together. In 2005 I proposed that our community (the 9 adults and our 10 children) leave for the developing world together to seek God and conceive of a new way of doing ministry. After a yearlong search we decided on Manila, Philippines. Many of us reference this experience throughout the book as it was such an essential 9 months of our lives together.

While in the Philippines we worked alongside Filipino church planters who worked exclusively in the slums. We lived among the poor in four side-by-side apartments, with no air conditioning and none of the comforts of home. We tested our communal bonds in the fire of ministry among the truly poor and we grew so much because of it. We will forever be in the debt of the Filipino leaders who taught us and guided us through that time. Our life together was less strange in Asia; people seemed to understand our commitment to each other and our collective sense of self. In many ways being in the Philippines felt like coming home. We discovered that most of the world does not strive so hard to remain isolated from each other and that sharing (life, possessions, purpose) is more the natural state of many cultures. We are unique in the world because we tend to see ourselves as a solo act and not an ensemble.

Too our surprise we also discovered that not only was our intentional community less strange, it was honored in Asia. People seemed to get it and even be inspired by it. We learned that our years of life together and the way we loved, trusted, confronted, and worked together was even an example to them. We realized that what we have been doing was so deeply biblical that it transcended our own culture. Maybe it could be for everyone.

We came back to Tampa in 2007 ready to begin again; starting a new missionary expression of church we called the Underground Network. Jason and Katy felt inspired to move out (they actually bought the half house--one of the original houses we lived in), and to start their own house church which was a huge success. Because they moved out, that made space for others. At the time of writing this forward, a dear friend Stacy has moved in, Joann married Chris and they are living in the house, and Jennifer is in the late stages of adopting a 16 year old. We are praying that we will add one more teenager to our mix.

Through it all, every Sunday night around 9pm we all gather in our living room. Jason and Katy come back over; Jeremy and Jessica pack up all their kids and put them down in our beds, as we all remember that we are a community not because we live together, but because our lives are intertwined.

There have been others through the years. Our home has always been a place of hospitality, especially to those in need. You may read references to some of the people to whom our home has been a sanctuary. Jason's sister Kim lived with us as she fought and lost a battle with cancer. Katy's sister Clare was a beloved part of our community for a couple of years. Macy, an 88 year old woman from the neighborhood that Monica befriended, lived with us until she was 92. Monica and I became therapeutic foster parents for a short time to a girl we had known from the neighborhood for years. So, while it sounds crowded, the truth is there is always room for one more. I hope this basic framework and timeline will help to put the content of this book into a context for you. Just like our home we are opening our lives to you in hopes that you will see yourself fitting in somewhere. That you will see we are all very different and yet we have all found something special together. Something that has too often eluded American Christians, but something we think is our birthright as the family of God. The rest of the book is about our journey in intentional community (one household) but the real treasure is not the sharing of a house. It is the sharing of ourselves. Welcome.

PART I

theory

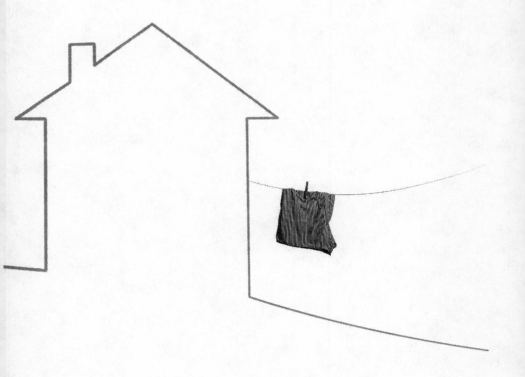

1
In Your Underwear:
Community as Exposure

It has happened only once. In more than 15 years of living with people who are not my family by blood, I have been caught in my underwear only once. I made a break for the bathroom very early one morning just as Crystal was walking out her bedroom door. First, I know this is a disturbing image to start with, but I really think it is the right one. Getting caught with your pants down, in a way, is what community is all about. And if you are already squeamish and can't handle it, I suggest you put this book down and spare yourself the anguish. If, on the other hand, you find my pantlessness funny or at least curious, then by all means read on.

Second, and in my defense, it was very early—like before 6 a.m. Maybe one day a year would someone in our house be awake at that unholy hour. Further, the distance between my door and the bathroom door was maybe 5 feet. What were the odds that I would get caught? I don't want to give you the impression I just hang out in my underwear, partly because that is disturbing but also because I don't. You can't do that when you live in community. Banish the thought. Our house is not some extension of our college dorm years or a hippy commune. (A commune, by the way, is by far the most common misperception about us, and still to this day I don't even know what a commune is.) We actually have a high value on modesty and privacy, higher than most. We have to so we can make it work. All my excuses aside, there I was, and there she was: horrified.

I told Monica, my wife, and she was mad (but not as mad as Crystal). She was hot. As with so many things, though, we worked it out—there was honesty, listening, understanding, apologies, and forgiveness. And the best thing of all, the thing that makes community and conflict so worth it all, in the end there was laughter.

Crystal could have thought (and maybe did), "Why do I put up with this? People running around the house in their underwear? It's ridiculous. I should just find my own place where I don't have to worry about walking outside my bedroom door to have my eyes assaulted by Brian in his underwear." Or I could have thought (although I didn't), "This is my house; why do I have to get harassed if I want to walk 5 feet to the bathroom in my underwear at 6 in the morning? I should just get my own place so I can walk around freely, maybe even watch TV or cook dinner in my underwear if I want." Instead, we laugh. And laugh. Every now and then when the time is right, my pain becomes everyone's joy, as we relive the episode. These are the moments we were made for, sinners enjoying the comedy of failure and forgiveness, the joy of reconciliation.

The Hope of Exposure

I think this story illustrates what we all decide to experience when we walk into community. We all must accept that we will get caught in our underwear. The journey into community must begin with the realization that we will all be exposed, that we will all feel vulnerable, and that we will all be subjected to the raw truth about each other. There are reasons people don't share who they really are. People tend to hide the truth about themselves because exposure would be both embarrassing and offensive. That is the nature of human beings. In a very real way, we ARE embarrassments to ourselves and an offense to others. We fear telling others the truth because the truth is ugly and because rejection is likely. We hide because we believe we will be able to preserve more relationships by projecting and protecting a false image of ourselves. I get it. But in community you kind of decide, "I am going to be exposed, and I am going to see if people will still want to be friends with me, if they will still love me once they know me."

What we have discovered after all these years is that not only do we choose to keep loving each other, but we also actually love each other more. Getting caught in your underwear is what makes community work. The longer we operate under pretense or false courtesy, the longer we put off real community. All communities are formed ultimately in their underwear. Until you get to that place of exposure, shock, and acceptance you are not really community. In his book *Life Together*, Dietrich Bonheoffer called it the shock of disillusionment. He argued that life together is not possible until you confront and progress beyond that moment when you say, "This stinks; this is not what I signed up for, and this is not community." In other words, we all enter into community with false expectations; the problem is we don't know what they are. Until those false expectations about what community is and who we are as individuals within it are released, there is no chance for real community.

The Challenge of Exposure

I have lived in intentional community for 15 years. I have helped to form dozens of similar communities in our city and around the country. I have walked with many of these communities through the predictable and healthy stages of conflict and development, so I can say with some confidence that community is awesome. But before it is awesome, it is hard.

You might be reading this book out of curiosity. Maybe someone you know has made the choice to live in intentional community, and you are trying to understand why. Maybe you are thinking about making this creative change to your lifestyle. Maybe you have started living with people, and you are desperate for help and direction. No matter the angle from which you consider intentional community, let's agree that it is a challenge. It is a challenge to our character, to our cultural sensibilities, to our profoundly ingrained and personal notions of space and property, and most of all to our sinfulness. But let me be clear: close-knit community challenges us in all the right ways. I want to be honest and admit it is hard, but I want to be equally straightforward that the bits of us that get challenged most are the bits that need confrontation.

Community is hard only because we like to hide and because we like to lie. Community is hard because we are (more than we like to admit) self-centered and arrogant. Even our insecurities and our dysfunctions are actually manifestations of our self-centeredness. Community is kind of like white blood cells for the soul. If you have no community in your life, you have no spiritual immune system. And isn't it painfully obvious when so many of Jesus' people seem to struggle with their character, mental health, and integrity in the same way as everyone else? It is not that Jesus doesn't make a difference; it is that the presence of Jesus often comes in the package of his people (his body), and we have tried to live more as individuals than as part of something.

The two great barriers to community are also the two big barriers to God in our lives: pride and insecurity. Most of us will find ourselves resisting community because of one of these internal arguments. You might be willing to be in your underwear, but you don't want to endure others in theirs. Conversely, you might be willing to allow others their exposure, but you will never let yourself appear that weak, that vulnerable. Can you tell which one comes from pride and which one is insecurity? They are strangely similar. In practice they accomplish the same thing: the constant work of the enemy, fragmentation.

We all need community, and in vulnerability we all are challenged. However, this book is about a certain permutation of community. This kind of community is not for everyone. Again, it is important from the outset to be clear that we are not making an argument that everyone should live this way or that the way we live is "real" community. Community, as I will explain later, is deeper and more important than where you live. I think that people can live very happy Christian lives in single-family dwellings.

Yet if you want to really know God, there are some aspects of what we do that you cannot avoid. Maybe in that way our story and our struggles can be a guide for anyone seeking any kind of community. I certainly hope so. But this book is really about life in what we call intentional community.

We say intentional, not accidental or necessary. Intentional. We could all live somewhere else, in some other way. But we choose to live the way we do, sometimes to the curiosity, reverence, or scorn of others. For all the reasons we have to live the way we do, for all the theological, economic, and even relational reasons, we mostly do it because we like it. I am not saying it is not a sacrifice; it is. I am not saying it is not prophetic; in many ways I think it is. I am not saying it is not practical, because it really is. But I don't think we would have made it this long together if it were not, at the end of the day, enjoyable.

The Joy of Exposure

From our perspective, it is just better to live this way. Now, it may be that we are just wired for this kind of thing. I have considered that. We have never tried to sell our way of life to others. We have never tried to imply that other people were wrong for living in their single-family dwellings. I do not believe that. What I am interested in doing is giving people the option to live another way. In other words, in Jesus we are all free to pursue community. What I don't like is the prescription from our culture that we HAVE to live in one way and are not free to live in another. I hope that by the end of reading this book you at least consider intentional community a biblical possibility and respect the people who choose to follow Jesus and pursue community in this way.

Living in single-family, detached housing is just one of those cultural assumptions people make without thinking about it, like going to college or learning to drive or wearing shoes. Everyone does it, and if you don't then maybe something is wrong with you. Like so many things cultural, we are free to live this way, but shouldn't we be free not to? As a Christian, I have to consider the call of Jesus on my life before the spoken and unspoken cultural demands made by the place where I was born. I mean, Jesus loved to call into question the socioreligious expectations made on people in his day. Shouldn't we?

Some people think that we are radicals. I am not really sure what that even means in the context of the Christian life. I think the whole thing is radical. Aren't we all radicals? As for the positive connotations, I am flattered, but I just don't think that something is particularly radical if it is mostly enjoyable. It might be different, but I am convinced that if every American Christian tried to live in an intentional community a lot of them—maybe even most—would like it. A community like ours enjoys a certain continuity with scripture and certain kinds of fruit that other Christians envy. We are not special; we are just normal people, like you. The difference is that we got it in our heads that because of Jesus, we were free—free to live inside or outside the culture. We are free to examine it, free to critique it, and of course free to change it. In many ways, not just in how we live, we are a counterculture community. We stand for a set of values that are rare and extraordinary.

We believe that, although we are given stewardship over our things, they ultimately and practically belong to God and therefore should be accessible to each other. We believe that we are people sent by God into the world he loves. We define ourselves by a commitment to him that is unwavering and undeniable, and that commitment extends to each other. But we are, in the end, pretty much like you. You will hear from all of us. The book itself is an exercise in community. We thought it would be cool to talk about this experience as a community or, better put, as individuals in community. So as you read through these chapters, see who you relate to. Maybe you are like Jessica, quiet but loyal, with a keen mind but a slow tongue. Or maybe you are like Crystal, creative, expressive, emotional, and always looking at the world in a unique way. Or maybe you are like me, talkative, confrontational, and idealistic. Read on and see.

The Enneagram

Some years ago, I stumbled on the enneagram. It is a fascinating personality typology that unlike other personality profiles acknowledges weakness in our types. I was particularly attracted to the notion that our personality type (the kind of person we are) is not always a good thing. The enneagram actually gives you a range. It explains possibilities for your type: when you are at your best, average, or worst. That rings more true to me than an explanation of myself that is only positive or neutral.

Once I found it, I thought it would be a good exercise for all of us to take that test together. So one night we all took it. We printed our results and started to share which type we all were. There are 9 adults in our community, and I thought this could give us real insight into not just ourselves but also how we interact as a group. One by one we shared, and after about the fifth or sixth person, I held my breath in disbelief. Sure enough, we were each a different type, 1–9. No repeating types at all. I still don't know if we were always these different types and God brought us together to make one unique whole, or if we were different when we met each other but over time have adapted to fill a space that was missing and not repeat something that was already there. Either way, you have to admit it is pretty cool/creepy/awesome.

So you will hear from each of us. The enneagram gave us new names and new categories for ourselves, but they are traits we always knew. I will use these type titles to introduce you to the community. From that vantage point, they will share about their experience of living in intentional community: what has been the most difficult for them, what has been the most rewarding, and how they have grown closer to Jesus living in community. Each person will share from his or her own point of view, and you may find that some of us seem strange and inscrutable to you while others finally make sense. That too will be a microcosm of what it is like to live in community. People are weird. You are too (if you're honest). But people are also amazing. What makes us different is what makes us endlessly frustrating but also what makes us invaluable to each other. Together, especially when there is mutual love and submission for Jesus and each other, we are unspeakably beautiful.

In the next two chapters I will lay some groundwork for understanding community in general. Then I will introduce you to members of my community: Jeremy the perfectionist, Jennifer the healer, Jason the achiever, Crystal the artist, Katy the investigator, Jessica the loyalist, Joann the enthusiast, Brian the challenger, and Monica the peacemaker. I love my community. I hope you will too. And we together hope that love will make you jealous for your own.

2
Paralyzed Friends:
Community and Jesus

A lot has been said and written about Jesus' personal commitment to ministry in community. But why did he do it that way? If there ever was a leader who simply did not need peers, advisors, or teammates, it was Jesus. A lot of the virtues of community have to do with the way it makes up for our weaknesses. We are undergirded by the health and strength of others, in all the places where we are unhealthy and weak. Jesus would have enjoyed none of those benefits of community, at least not in some moral sense. He was, after all, perfect, yet in his perfection he chose community anyway.

Jesus is the consummate teacher; everything he does has pedagogical value. The incarnation itself is a lesson about life and the value of human beings. So for Jesus, who did not need a team, to choose to do ministry within the context of a team invites a second look at community itself. What is it about life in community that is simply better than life alone?

There are so many access points for us to consider community and its theological significance in the New Testament. There is, for example, Jesus' relationship with the disciples, their relationships with each other, the Book of Acts, and ecclesiology. Yet I find that I draw more and more meaning lately from the more obscure references Jesus makes toward community. Stories that don't even appear on the surface to be about community but maybe are. I like the story of the paralytic, as told by Luke (Luke 5:17–26).

In this short but remarkable story, Jesus is said to be teaching in someone's home. As usual, he has drawn a crowd, and the house is filled with people—so full in fact that people are not really able to get in or out. Luke tells us that some friends of a paralytic man were trying to get their friend in to see Jesus. Presumably they had heard the rumors that Jesus could bend the natural world to his will, that he had the power to heal their friend.

These rumors were of course true, so they try furiously to get in to see Jesus. The crowd is simply too much. It is interesting how the effect of too many people is sometimes the same as too few: isolating. It is not clear how they come to the idea, but consensus builds around the possibility of getting on top of the house and digging a hole in the thatch and mud roof. No act of vandalism has ever seemed so noble or been more celebrated than this one. I sometimes think about the owner of the house and how he must have felt about all this. He couldn't have been as pleased with the idea.

I guess in all the commotion of Jesus teaching, no one notices as they dig this hole and begin lowering their paralyzed friend down into the middle of the house. Jesus stops his teaching (kind of hard not to) and addresses the paralyzed man. The first significant oddity of the interaction is that Jesus calls this man "Friend." He does not refer to anyone else in the gospel directly as friend, and it appears to me that Jesus has sized this man up in a way that we might have missed. Maybe Jesus calls this man friend because he understands the unique beauty of the thing they have all just witnessed. Who is this man who has such friends? Luke says, "When he saw their faith." It is a community that brings the man to Jesus, it is a community that has faith together for a miracle, and it is a community that Jesus responds to.

If you were paralyzed in the first-century world, you were almost certainly doomed to a life of poverty, begging, and alienation from others. But this guy not only has friends but the kind we all wish we could have. He has the kind of friends it is not even clear at this point if Jesus has.

At the end of his life, when Jesus was most vulnerable, all of his friends ran away, afraid to suffer alongside him. But this nameless paralytic has the kind of friends who don't just carry him; they tear through buildings, break the law, and generally embarrass themselves for the sake of their friend. Maybe Jesus calls him friend because that is the overwhelming reality of that moment. A friend, in the company of his friends, doing the best that friendship can do, bearing burdens, and seeking wholeness together.

The second significant oddity in the story is that Jesus does not offer this man healing. He offers him forgiveness. I don't know how you feel about that, but I guess if I am honest I would be a little frustrated by that. If I am one of the friends, I am thinking, "Um, okay, thank you for the forgiveness and all that. Not that we are ungrateful for your offer of religious stuff; we are, but we didn't come here because he is a sinner. We came here because he can't walk."

If the first comment is reference to the community that exists with this man and his friends, the second is a reference to the community that does not exist between the man and God. It is as if Jesus has two concerns for the man (maybe for every man): that he would have healthy, reconciled, deeply loving (sacrificial) community with other human beings; and that he would have the same with the God who made him. He sees and comments that he has the first. I imagine Jesus smiling as he calls the man friend but frowning as he recognizes he lacks the second. So Jesus, in one declaration, restores that most important of all relationships; he restores him to God.

The story is about community because it is community that got the man into the presence of Jesus, it is the man's community that impresses Jesus, and it is restored community with the Father that Jesus offers the man. Jesus seems more than content with the transaction, as if he has left nothing of real value out.

Jesus' detractors, who are also present, scoff at the theological inappropriateness of Jesus claiming to forgive the man's sin. So in response to them, to prove a point to his critics, Jesus heals the guy. Which is harder, he asks, to say your sins are forgiven, or to get up and walk? To prove that he can say the former, he says and demonstrates the power to say the latter. In the flow of the story, however, it is the community with God that is the real and lasting miracle.

Community and the Nature of God

It is important to consider the theological back story here. We have the improved perspective to begin to understand what even the audience then could not have fully understood: God is a community. That is to say, he is three as much as he is one. The mystery of the trinity is that God exists, within the wonder and transcendence of his nature, as three persons. That means he is a community. It actually begins to explain why we all have such a longing for community. Since we were made in the image of the triune God, we long for the wholeness and community that God experiences within himself.

God is complete in that he has, within his person, the virtues of love, deference, listening, service, sacrifice, and even submission. When you think about the relationship that Jesus has with the Father as an internal relationship, you begin to see the possibilities of holy community. We are like God in that we were made for those same virtues. His fingerprints are still on us, in spite of our disregard for his ways. Still, to return to God means a return to the holiness and to the wholeness of community.

When God created human beings he created us as us, male and female, not choosing to contain his divine image to just one gender. And from the beginning we were created to reflect his nature, as community. The only hiccup in the creation narrative of Genesis 1 is when Adam was created but stood in the vast beauty and wonder of nature, alone. It was not then, in the perfection of Eden, and it is not now, in the chaos of Babylon, good for man to be alone.

Community and the Image of God

Human beings thrive in community; in collaboration we are at our best. Conversely, our greatest evils as a people are produced by isolation and the fragmentation of human community. The kiss of God upon our souls was community, and the curse of sin and our partnership with evil is fragmentation. The great work of the enemy in the world is the work of fracturing, dividing, and breaking. The enemy cannot—like God and like you and I (who are made in the image of God)—create. The enemy can corrupt only what is created. He can only fragment it, breaking it into less and less glorious, God-revealing pieces. This is, grossly stated, what the devil does in the world.

God, on the other hand, who first gave us community with each other and with him, is at work also in the world. His work is to heal, reconcile, and restore what is broken, fragmented, and fractured into what it was intended to be. Simply put, God makes things whole again. The recent theological interest in the Hebrew notion of shalom (often translated peace) has become a helpful rubric for the intention of God in the world. The term is richer and deeper than that one English connotation, as it actually sounds the depths of the human longing not just for the end of hostility (peace) but also for the restoration of all things to their intended state, wholeness, and harmony with God and others.

The hope of human beings and the mission of God, it could be said, is to bring peace to the hostility of the enemy and wholeness to all that is broken. The New Testament equivalent of shalom is what Jesus called the kingdom of God. It is not just a spiritual or a political reign. So sweeping and comprehensive, the term is meant to include all things. It is, again, the healing of every world system and every broken thing in the universe. It is that significant.

The dream of the kingdom of God is a dream of community, and the good news of the kingdom of God is what Paul called "the message of reconciliation" (2 Corinthians 5:19). Jesus came to accomplish the dual purpose of reconciliation (reconciling the world to God and people to each other) and to destroy all the works of the evil one (1 John 3:8). The death and resurrection of Jesus accomplishes both because reconciliation means the end of division and all its permutations in the world.

Authority in Community

Maybe Jesus is inspired by the community of the paralytic because he recognizes his own handiwork when he sees it. He sees that something very like the kingdom is happening among these friends. Again, he is moved when he sees their communal faith—the faith of not just the man but of his whole community. God knows us together; he sees and responds to us together. In another place, Jesus would teach that when two of us agree on anything in his name, it will be heard and done by the Father (Matthew 18:19).

In my circles, that always seems to be applied to prayer, and maybe that is what Jesus meant. But he does not choose to use the word prayer. He does not say "when two of you pray about something," or "ask in prayer." He says agree. I find that very meaningful for our understanding of community. There is power in numbers.

I have six children. If one of them asks me for something that seems frivolous or unnecessary, I am likely to say no. Sometimes I am even tempted to just dismiss the request. Every once in a while they conspire together, talking, planning, agreeing on something. That agreement can be very powerful and beautiful as an act of community for them. They hear each other's excitement for a thing, and it grows. More than that, their sense of connection with each other grows until they bring their agreement to me or Monica. I have to admit, it is a powerful thing to see your children all in agreement about something, and it is very difficult to deny them. Likewise, when the people of God are in agreement about something that is also in the name and nature of Jesus to grant, it will happen.

In my experience, Christians underestimate the power they have individually. In scripture, having the authority of Jesus and the presence of the Holy Spirit inside us gives us access to almost unthinkable power.

Healing the sick or dying, predicting the future, supernatural knowledge of the past, and the miraculous are all within the normative experience of a believer. This is who we are alone. But when we work together, when we collaborate, when our faith is exercised in agreement with one another, in the name of Jesus—no wonder Jesus said, "I will build my church and the gates of Hell will not prevail against it." We are immeasurably more powerful in Jesus than we are without him, and I believe we are exponentially more powerful in the community of Jesus than alone.

There are three deeply important truths that I see in the community of the paralyzed friend; they provide a kind of value system for us as we consider the practice of intentional community. If you are going to enter into it, I suggest you consider carefully these lessons.

Lesson One: The deepest community forms around the struggle to stand in the presence of Jesus.

Before we are community, we are Christian. The primacy of Jesus is everything in healthy community. If people understand their community as somehow coming before or taking the place of Jesus in their lives, they are in serious trouble. Not only is that idolatry, but it will also induce all kinds of dysfunctions and even abuse. We were made for God before we were made for community. The strongest communities understand that they are all on the same journey toward Jesus and into his mission. Communities that place the group in the seat of primacy will succumb to someone else's control.

Human beings were meant to pursue God together and not alone, but it is God who is the pursuit, not the company we keep on the journey. We cannot fully understand and experience the love, grace, and presence of Jesus in the world without community. We are, for each other, the body of Jesus. So while we do not want to put community in the place of Jesus, we need each other to fully experience him. The key is primacy. Jesus is first. His call, his voice, and his leading are always the goal. When we understand that God uses community to speak to us or to confirm what we are hearing, then we are in a strong position. On the other hand, when we stop praying and listening to God, acquiescing to the will of the community and in our laziness assuming that is the voice of God, then we have lost our way.

The friends of the paralytic struggle and overcome the obstacles to getting in the presence of Jesus. Presumably none of them could have gotten there alone—certainly not the paralytic. Maybe the others could have alone, but if they were going to get him in there they had to go together. These friends discover their interdependence as they lower their weakest member into the presence of Jesus, which leads us to lesson two.

Lesson Two: Great communities are built around their weakest members.

I believe that societies, which are really just the largest formations of human community, can be judged by how they treat their weakest members. For some, it is their children or the poor in their midst or, like this man, people with disabilities. It is an important rubric for those of us who love Jesus. He was more than fond of the weakest people in society. He slowed down and built his ministry around them.

I think that Jesus is showing us something about greatness. To be great is to be willing to become weak. In the incarnation Jesus becomes weak. He willingly gives up his place of strength and comfort to become one of us, to enter into the pain, the frailty, the humiliation of being a human being. In Jesus, God suffers the indignity of the incarnation only to live a life of obscured greatness. Jesus was shy. Always he chose the low seat; always he masked his true identity and massive power. Always he held his tongue. And because of that restraint and modesty he felt most at home in the company of the sick and sinners. It is as if he had come all this way to be with the weak, and nothing was going to stop him from finishing that journey.

As I have said, within the mystery of the trinity there is love, sacrifice, and even submission. Because of the incarnation, Jesus becomes the weakest member of the triune community. Jesus takes on human nature and human sin and eventually death itself and in so doing fasts from his Godhood. Jesus is God become paralyzed. There are things he should know but doesn't. Things he should be able to do but can't. Even his will is no longer free; he subjugates it completely to the Father, all to show us how to be human. God becomes human to show us how to love and submit to him. God becomes weak, paralyzed, to show us how to be weak.

It is precisely because of this act of lowering that Jesus is finally exalted. Philippians 2 describes what Daniel saw centuries before and what John would envision decades later in Revelation 4: the transfer of honor and power and authority to Jesus. The weakest, exactly because he was the weakest, becomes the most honored. Within the trinity Jesus is the weakest member, and therefore he becomes the center of the revelation of the power of God. The authority that has always been the Father's becomes his; there is a shift. The Father now honors the Son, and the spirit glorifies the Son. And in all of this mutual honoring there is never loss or competition. There is no diminishment of the Father to give his authority to the Son; it is his pleasure to do so.

As the perfect example of community, God teaches us that our shadow versions of God's own relationship with himself, our communities, should also revolve around the weakest member.

Lesson Three: Deep communities work together toward the goal of healing.

I will talk more about this in Chapter 12, but it should be noted here as well that great communities do not simply live together but also work together toward something. Mission is a critical part of being a healthy community. Mission is what feeds us; it is what challenges us. Human beings need to fight something. The closer you get to Jesus, the more you are affected by a deep spiritual discontentment, the more you become dissatisfied with the way things are. What drives these friends to break into another man's house is that they are tired of their friend's limitations. They know it is not right, not the way God intended him to be, and they want healing. That angst was meant to be channeled into mission. We want things to change because God wants things to change. When communities neglect mission, all of that angst, frustration, and desire to fight something gets turned inward.

My family and I recently returned from a vacation to discover that we had forgotten to ask someone to feed our fish. I don't really know anything about fish, so I was mortified to hear that, in the absence of a food source, the fish had started to eat each other. More to the point, the bigger fish ate the smaller, weaker ones. This is a graphic but accurate depiction of Christians who are not fed by the challenge of mission. When we are not focusing our holy discontent on the work of the enemy (we do not wrestle against flesh and blood), we tend to focus on what is closest to us—other Christians. All of us know what it looks like when Christians turn against each other. The problem is not that they just need to work harder to get along; the problem is that they are not spent from the war against evil. They have too much energy and time on their hands.

One of the reasons I don't pick on the flaws of my community is because I am too tired. We are busy trying to accomplish something with our lives; the gospel's call is too great and costs us everything. We do not have the energy to look for petty faults in each other. On the contrary, I need to fall back into my community like a soft bed at the end of a hard day's work, to be with people who understand our common struggle for the kingdom and against darkness. The people of Jesus look very beautiful if you have spent the day wrestling with the devil. However, if you don't ever walk into darkness you will inevitably occupy your time and energy with the shadows and minor flaws of your friends, and it is always the weakest that gets eaten first.

Our hope in community is to follow Jesus and to walk with each other as we follow him. It is my deep and persistent conviction that as we do that, showing love and respect to each other and the teacher who called us, we will all receive healing. We don't pursue our own healing directly, but as we offer healing to others we find we are being healed as well.

3
Fried Eggs:
Community as Shared Life

For all the years I have lived in intentional community, I have rarely defined what we are doing for anyone. I rarely speak in public about it, and when I do, I don't call people to live as we do. Instead, I call people into deeper relationships of love, honor, and accountability with each other. We all need deep Christian community, but it does not have to look like shared living space. Yet some of us who live this way have come to talk about "living in community" as if it were synonymous with the more critical spiritual discipline of community. It is not. For us, though, the choice to live in intentional community is so intertwined with the pursuit of biblical community (as a principle) that we have trouble delineating. All throughout this book you will notice we cannot seem to separate them. If you live in intentional community, there is no conflict; if, however, you are reading this book looking for community without living together, it is possible. For that reason, I have had to do more thinking on what is essential community. What is it that we all need? What is community really? And how does living together offer us the possibility of community but is not itself the goal?

Community as a Bounded Set

The term bounded set comes from mathematics. Simply put, it is a series or group of numbers connected by some mathematical feature.

All the numbers share the same mathematical space. There is a way of looking at community that is like a bounded set. This view of community defines it from an external perspective. That is, community is something that you can discern by looking at it and define by its features. A bounded set could be a family, or members of the same gym, or a soccer team. A bounded set would include your coworkers, a bible study group, or the people who live in your house. It could be that when we think of community we are thinking about being in the same space with the same people. When we define community this way, the application becomes obvious: get into the same space as often and as closely as possible.

If you are a student at a major university, you are then a member of that bounded set. But 30,000 members hardly make community achievable as an ideal. So we narrow the set. Maybe being a member of the basket-weaving club sufficiently narrows the set. So we might form a smaller group bound not only by being students of the university but also by being lovers of basket weaving. The problem with this view is that community is not simply about location. That is to say, community does not happen just because we have space or affinity in common. Neighborhoods are good examples.

Most neighborhoods in America are composed of people who are, for the most part, strangers to one another. Simply because they live on the same street and even share the same concerns does not mean that they have community with one another. In a secular sense, community has been defined this way. We can be a part of a community, and actually know no one in it. I could be a member of the university community or the local neighborhood community simply because I am there. Being members of the bounded set is more about space and location than it is about some expression of intimacy and relationship.

Obviously this cannot be our definition of community, yet it has had its influence. Sometimes when we think about community we think of the closest bounded set we can imagine. Perhaps some people think about my lifestyle of intentional residential community, of families and singles living under the same roof. For me, a monastery comes to mind. But even monks who live with a vow for brotherhood and prayer and isolation to the outside world do not have community with each other just because they enter the monastery. They can quarrel or ignore each other just as well as the rest of us. We are tempted by this view because it is simple, manageable. Leaders in particular are going to be attracted to a more concrete definition of community, always asking themselves the questions, "Are we community or not?" And we feel like one of the things we can control is getting people into the same location. So we go on thinking of community as a group of people who meet or see each other regularly and who have common interests. Given this definition of community, the goal becomes clear: meet more often and have more things in common. However, this is not the goal of biblical community.

Some of us know this from experience. People who live together, even in religious communities, do not necessarily experience community. But all of us know this. We all find ourselves in multiple bounded set groups, but does that mean we have community with them? If you are in a sports league or in a bible study group or at an office with coworkers, does that mean you experience community with them? I once stayed in a monastery where the monks kept a vow of silence, yet the abbot explained to me that there was deep infighting among the brothers and that some were divided from the others. The snub of not speaking to each other took on a whole new meaning in this strange and extremely bounded context. Since even monks can avoid the experience of community, the bounded set must not be enough. It might be a prerequisite for community, but it alone is not community.

Swimming

Just like you need water to go swimming, you also need relationships and intimacy to experience community. Just because you are in water does not mean you are swimming. In fact, some people, when thrown into the water, discover quickly they have never learned to swim, so they never venture into the depths where they cannot stand. Most bounded sets keep us relating to each other in the shallow end. We don't know how to swim so we never venture deeper, even though we are in water. We rely on the space and location of the relationships because we do not know how to swim in the depths of a kind of community the bible calls koinonia. Even though we inhabit the same space where community is possible, we don't really know how to enter into it.

Community as an Ideal

The other important misrepresentation of community, which will be critical to forging a working definition, is to think of it as an ideal. In this way, we see community as something to be achieved and, in one sense, something that never will be. Ideals are by nature elusive and intangible. They draw us out but are never really accomplished. We think of ideals in terms of a continuum. If we were to create a continuum for community, we would then plot ourselves (or our group) somewhere between isolation and true community.

Isolation   Community

We invariably try to plot ourselves on the continuum. We take the groups to which we belong and measure or score our progress. The problem with this view is that, again, we see community as something that just needs the right parts, as accessories to be added. When the ideal view of community is coupled with the bounded set concept, we can set up a new legalism for community and miss the truer spiritual nature of biblical community. Plus, plotting ourselves on some idealistic continuum leads us to feel like community is something that we can never actually achieve; we can only come closer. However, this is not the impression the bible gives.

Biblical koinonia is something that God makes possible for his people. It is a gift he gives that is accessible not only for every group of Christians but also for every Christian within that group. If we think of community only as an ideal, then, like perfection, it becomes a concept that will serve only to frustrate us and will actually become a stumbling block for our groups. When community is seen only as something that we never quite are, we can become discouraged by the journey toward it and over time give up trying to achieve it. Further, when it is seen as some ideal that we never live up to we can actually use it against each other as a kind of criticism. Ironically, this ends up keeping us from both appreciating the fellowship we have and pursuing a deeper, more frequent experience.

Community as Shared Life

As I have wondered about and tried to live "in community," I have learned a number of things. First, living with other people does not necessarily mean you are experiencing community with them. Second, living with certain people does not mean that you cannot experience community with others outside that living arrangement. Third, I have learned that community is really measured by moments and is too spiritual to confine to one decision we make or don't make.

The word that is translated community in the New Testament is the word koinonia. It is also translated fellowship or communion. These synonyms can help us to free up the concept a little bit. Fellowship, we know is possible with any believer, anywhere in the world at any time. If I travel to another country and meet a pastor or another leader, I can have real and significant fellowship with him or her. I know this because I have experienced it many times. I will never make a choice to live with this person, to work for the same ministry or even to collaborate on the same project. But in a very real sense we can discover together that we are in fact family, siblings of the same Father and called together to the same global mission. With this person whom I will share precious little time, I can have community. I'm sure you know what it's like to see friends after having not seen them for months or even years; when you do, it is like you pick up right where you left off. Because you love and trust them, the barriers come down immediately, and you immediately experience the deepest kind of community.

Perhaps a more helpful construct, the idea of communion, is the idea of sharing. If we commune with someone, if we have communion, it means that we have shared something deeply. The Lord's Supper has come to be called communion precisely because we recognize that to symbolically partake of the body and blood of Jesus is to share something with him. It is a communion of the saints who partake and the God who offers his own body as the ritual meal. Communion is sharing. If we see community as sharing some part of our lives with each other, then we realize that it does not have to be confined by one particular bounded set and that it is an ideal that can be realized and measured from one moment to the next.

Whether I am in a small group, a meeting, with a friend, or spending the weekend with my family, community is something that I have to pursue as a spiritual possibility, an achievable ideal. I might set up the perfect vacation for my friends or my family; all the pieces are in place for real sharing, openness, and community, but then it does not seem to happen. We have to look for the opportunities and then seize them. We have to acknowledge real sharing when it is happening. We have community because we realize we can.

Toward a Definition

Community is when our lives mysteriously overlap with one another. It is when my concerns, my joy, my fear, my hopes are for one moment in time your concerns, your joy, fear, or hope. It is something that happens because we want it to happen and because we look for it. It is possible when we let down our guards, when we allow each other's questions and interest to penetrate our self-protection mechanisms and we really share who we are.

Some of the most profound community that I have ever experienced has been through laughter—not just finding the same thing funny but sharing laughter as a kind of medicine for our souls. Being willing to just laugh with someone, to the point where it hurts your stomach, in the vulnerability that comes from not needing to be the center, but by all agreeing that something is very funny and that joy is needed, is community. It is community because it is soul agreement. In this way, community is possible only when there is at least some vulnerability. We can share ourselves, our lives, only when we offer something of ourselves and our lives to each other.

Eggs

The brilliant Filipina theologian Melba Maggay explained to us when we lived in the Philippines that a bounded set is like a pot or a pan. You can put a bunch of eggs in the same pot, cook them, or boil them, and at the end all you have are a pot full of individual eggs. There is no overlap, no sharing. The shells assure that. Too often we have tried to have community with each other by getting into the same pot, even cooking or going through something together. But we avoid vulnerability and keep our shells intact. Perhaps from the outside it looks like community. "Hey, look at those eggs; they have so much in common. They all live in the same pot; they were all cooked in the same water…" You get the point.

Now think of a frying pan as your bounded set. Being in the same space as we have already established is not enough, but you can hardly have intimacy with someone without it. This time you crack the eggs. As each egg is placed in the pan and the heat is turned up, the eggs touch and overlap one another. The whites of the eggs are shared, and the edge of one egg is the same as the edge of another. The group of eggs is still a group of eggs, but the eggs are also now one new thing as well.

Created as Individuals, Called into Community

To understand how we can be a collective we have to first understand and appreciate how we are not. God created us as individuals. We can lament our lack of community and blame our fiercely individualistic culture—certainly that has not helped us—but every human being was created as a functioning individual. Biologically, mentally, even spiritually we are individuals, and God made us that way. This is yet another paradox we have to appreciate. God is not asking us to stop being individuals. Not if he made us that way. God gave each of us freedom, and that gift cannot be taken away by any government or church or leader or even community. But he has also called us into community. The gift of individuality is darkened by sin, and we can no longer be trusted to walk alone. We need each other as an extension of our need for God. We are created as individuals but called by God into community with each other. Certainly some of our individuality should be submitted in humility to others, but never sacrificed. We are who we are, and our greatest task in life is to become the person God designed and intended us to be. Nothing more and nothing less.

Family

Even in a family I realize that we are all a collection of individuals. I go to work each day, my kids go to their schools and Monica has her set of responsibilities. We are a family. We live in the same house, we share the same name, but we are individuals. We all have our own lives. Perhaps more importantly, we all have our own minds. Even my 2 year old is profoundly unique and self-contained. He is a walking, talking ego. If we have ever been told we think we are "the center of the universe," it has been as an insult. But isn't that, in a very real sense, what we are to ourselves? Not as a spiritual reality (nothing could be further from the truth) but in terms of vantage point. Isn't that true? I see the world as an individual. Sharing thoughts with another person without words (telepathy) is so foreign to us as human beings that is it the stuff of science fiction. When I acknowledge that I am an individual and take responsibility for that and realize that my kids or my friends are also individuals, then I see what a challenge and what a wonder the experience of community can be.

I can sit all day with one of my daughters, but that does not mean she will tell me what she is really thinking. I can play catch a thousand times with my boys, and that does not mean that they will trust me the first time they are interested in a girl. Community is something that I have to look for and seize with my kids when I have the chance. It is not a given. We have to have time together for that to happen. But time is not the commodity. Community is.

Back to the Frying Pan

Community is the overlapping of our lives, the momentary and profound overlapping of our individual lives with each other. The white part of the egg becomes indistinguishable on the edges. The eggs share the white part together, but their individuality (in the yoke) stays intact. We are still all distinguishable from one another. We are a community of individuals. We share because we know who we are. We can really share our lives with each other only when we are aware of who we are. In this way, community is affirming to both the collective and the individual. When community is happening we feel more whole as individuals. It is not a loss of individuality but a profound affirmation of who we are. Ironically, it is isolation that destroys us as individuals and community that most affirms us.

When I share something painful with a friend and he shares that pain with me, we have fellowship, community. I walk away from that experience less afraid of my fears or my pain. My friend helps me make sense of that pain and understand who I am and who I am not in the midst of it. I am more whole as an individual because I was vulnerable and shared my pain with another. It is the same for anguish, joy and laughter, love and romance and hope, and anxiety and everything else. When we think of community this way it changes how we pursue it. This frees us from definitions of community that are too legalistic or narrow. We know that community is something that we can have (or not have) with every believer. It puts the burden of work on sharing and on looking for ways to give ourselves to each other. We know that gathering regularly or living together may make this more likely or more doable, but the gathering itself is not a substitute for the spiritual reality of communion with each other. Also, when we think of community this way it changes the way we think about conflict and unity.

Conflict and Unity

One of the paradoxical tensions of community is the call to both biblical unity and biblical confrontation. Since sin and selfishness are too often welcomed guests in our community relationships, confrontation is and always will be necessary for community to stay healthy. The idea of accountability may sound more palatable, but the truth is that accountability is nothing without the possibility of confrontation. Since confrontation is such a neglected art, Christians, like everyone else, often find themselves inept for the task.

Too often confrontation is brought with pride and ignorance. The person doing the confrontation cannot fail to love and hide behind the sin of the accused. Even when the person being confronted is clearly in the wrong, confrontation has to be marshaled in humility, since the people confronting are themselves also sinners and will themselves one day be in need of mercy. Often many of the problems that occur in confrontation could be avoided if those who are bringing the word of correction would pursue it with genuine love for the person and authentic humility about themselves.

The other problems occur when confrontation is met with pride and a failure to acknowledge loving correction. This dynamic we more readily understand. Too often we meet correction with defensiveness, blaming, and a big dose of denial. A loving community and strong friendships should be able to patiently and carefully penetrate these defense mechanisms. Indeed, one of the real gifts of meaningful friendships is the safety and accountability of confrontation. We need to have confrontation, but we do not need to have conflict. Conflict is inevitable only because too often sin in the group is met with more sin. Conflict happens when sin in the group is coupled with pride when it is confronted (in the confronters or in the confronted). This is where the complementary value of unity becomes vital to the tension of community.

While addressing sin in others is a necessary part of accountable, strong friendships, unity is equally if not more necessary. Like families, some communities are conflict averse and do everything they can to avoid it, including neglecting necessary confrontation. But like other families, some communities are conflict seeking. They do not shy away from conflict (which is a strength) but do not value unity with the same fervor. I know that was a flaw of my leadership in the early years of our community. Sometimes the substance of our confrontation is not sin at all but personal preferences colliding or the exaggeration of the effect of a sin. Further, the people who are wired to more fully appreciate unity, the peacemakers, are not valued as they should be and in the worst cases are seen as hindrances to "true community." As if true community were measured in conflict.

Consequently, those who would like to minimize conflict are sometimes seen as weak or less committed to the process of community. Sometimes the loving thing to do is to overlook a minor offense or to offer forgiveness that has not been asked for or, even more importantly, to acknowledge that we could be wrong in our appraisal of the error itself. The love of unity requires the ability and capacity to see things from another perspective—more than that, to appreciate that perspective, even to try it on, to step into the other person's shoes and to value where he or she is coming from.

Sometimes conflict has to happen because there is sin in the community that needs to be confronted. But sometimes peace has to happen because there is sin in the community that needs to be confronted with peace.

I have seen communities that have become addicted to conflict with each other. I know that no one reading this will assume that this refers to their community, but consider it. If a group (or any relationship for that matter) knows intimacy only through conflict and values conflict (whether spoken or not) as the highest expression of true community, does it not stand to reason that the group will maintain a steady diet of conflict? And when there is peace, will they not feel as though they are failing at community? Whether a conflict is warranted becomes something that the group cannot distinguish. If there is a problem, the group simply has no other way to deal with it besides confrontation. And there is always a problem. In many ways community is built as much on what is not said as on what is said. If you are new to community, learn from my mistakes: you need both people who bring confrontation and people who seek to avoid it. Only when both concerns are held in tension is healthy community possible.

The dilemma for us comes in the realization that we cannot seem to have peace, only conflict. These communities are poisoned by the upholding of only one value in the paradox. Confrontation, which is necessary but which should be rare, becomes the norm. And peace, which is also necessary but which should be the basic common experience, becomes rare and difficult to achieve for even one evening. Maybe it is okay to think about spending less of your time in that context and more with other friends.

A Fresh Start

It could be seen as a breach of community to leave one group and to start another. Certainly, when community is healthy and functioning for the good of everyone in it, it would be strange for someone to walk away. I have long thought that the only Christlike reason to leave a community setting is for the sake of mission. We should really leave one community in favor of another only when we believe God is both calling us and when we believe we will be more effective.

If a couple in my community senses God calling them to become missionaries to another nation, shouldn't we all rejoice with them and help them pack? Jason and Katy, both contributors to this book and both housemates of our community for more than a decade, recently sensed God's call to plant a new ministry in Germany. It was the community that affirmed that call. And even though we are all experiencing the pain of seeing them go, we are for them. In a way that transcends where they live. If we did not believe it was right for them to go, they likely wouldn't, trusting us as confidants and counselors. When God is speaking to them, we too can hear the voice of the shepherd calling them; we confirm that it is his word to them, and they go with our love and blessing.

Likewise, when God calls us to subtler, shorter journeys, we should still look to celebrate that transition and bless it if at all possible. It is conceivable that community can be strained by relationships that just do not seem to be working. This may be because of sin or just because of personality, but I am not sure it really matters. We should bear with one another. If instead we find ourselves in constant conflict and unable to cooperate well with the people around us, we should find a place where we can.

It is conceivable that a person could walk out on healthy community because he or she is running away from something. However, being free to leave community is anything but a breach of community; it is its hallmark. Healthy families consist of children who want to grow up and one day leave the house and parents who want the same thing for them. Healthy families are good models of community in that the spiritual parents should likewise desire to see their spiritual children grow up and move on to new things.

Part of what I am proposing is a redefining of community that allows for the expansion of our concept of who is "in" and who is "out." Where we have narrowly defined community as a small group or a household, we have risked becoming too rigid and exclusivist. When it is time for people to move on or to form new communities, we assume that they are "leaving" community with us. We need a new definition of community that allows these people to remain in meaningful relationship with us. Further, we have not reached out the way we should because we have too narrowly defined the people with whom we are "in community." We have not always had room in our lives or in our hearts for strangers or new friends.

Seeing community as more of an organic gift, we can begin to look for it everywhere we meet people. Our communities should be like rivers, always flowing with people (in and out of our meetings) but always connected by the current itself. When small groups become preoccupied with conflict and cannot live in peace and joy with one another, members should be free to look for new expressions of community with more than just those particular people. The irony is that if we allow our relationships to grow and mature and change in submission to God's Spirit, the change will bring us into deeper community. Sometimes someone moving out of a live-in community environment but staying connected relationally may produce peace and thus save the relationship and allow for more genuine community to occur.

I am going to continue living with other Christians. The benefits are very real and very holy for us. But I refuse to categorize our choice as the only Godly choice. More than that, I want to affirm every believer's calling to seek Jesus on where and how and with whom they should live. It can be a complicated decision when we have models that all seem good for different reasons. This is why we need God. In this, as in all things, we have to take very seriously the work of prayer and the submission of our whole lives to Jesus. Our goal in writing this book is to give people the freedom to choose to live together or not. We just want readers to know that the former is a biblical option. Some of us should find friends who we love and move in with them, for the sake of the common ministry we are called to, for the sake of friendship and accountability, and for the fun of it. Others of us should consider living near our closer friends, seeing them less frequently but meaningfully as often as we can. Still others will find that personal space helps them or their family really commit and will experience community in their home church or ministry environment when they are there. The goal is sharing life, from one moment to the next. I cannot prescribe what decision you should make. But each of these could be the right thing or the wrong thing for you. The key is to ask God. He knows you best.

PART II
experience

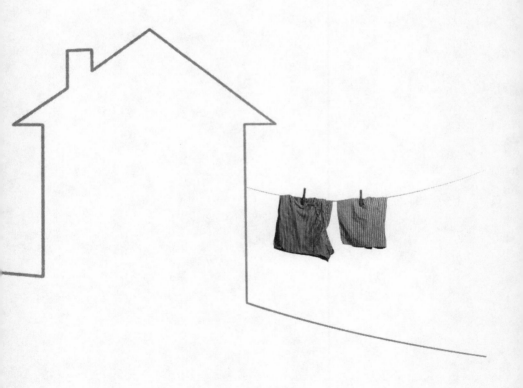

4
TYPE ONE:
The Reformer/Perfectionist
Jeremy Stephens

The Rational, Idealistic Type:
Principled, Purposeful, Self-Controlled, and Perfectionistic

I've cooked thousands of hamburgers in my life. Literally thousands. It's part of the job description for college ministry. If you want to meet new people on campus, food is a must. So every August, I cooked hundreds of hamburgers in my backyard, and every year I was driven to improve and refine the process. One year, in an effort to become more efficient, I invited some other leaders, David, Ray, and Will, over to my house with their propane grills. I supplied the burgers, and we cooked together. We tried to contain the grease that dripped from the meat by laying aluminum foil underneath the grills. What we didn't consider was how quickly the grease collecting in the foil would ignite into an uncontrollable fire. Flames spilled out of the bottom of the grill toward the propane tank, and an explosion seemed inevitable. These are the moments you discover what kind of person you are. As we watched the tank ignite, David and I immediately jumped back screaming and holding onto each other. Ray stood there petrified, but Will calmly walked over to the hose, turned it on, and washed away the flames. Any of us could have done it, but only Will had the presence of mind to do it.

If you are a reformer like me, living in community will be an exercise in needing other people. You may never know exactly how or when you will need them, but you will. At some point in your life a propane tank will be on fire, and you will need others to deal with it or suffer the explosion. I've seen many believers trying to follow Jesus with all the right books and religious activities, but they lack community. They isolate themselves until their lives become so tangled that they have to ask for help. Reformers, in particular, seem to think all of their decisions are right. In many cases, they can make isolated decisions about every area of their lives as if they don't need anyone else and then wonder how they found themselves feeling distant from God and alone. Mine is a story of a raging perfectionist who tried to improve the world but realized in his community that he needed to be saved from himself.

Community Has Healed Me

I am driven to perfection and to reforming thoughts, systems, and actions in myself and others. As part of my addiction to improvement, I create systems and structures to contain life into organized, controlled, and efficient units. I can't help thinking about how to do it better next time: a better meal, meeting, class, conversation, or date. What's the most effective way to drive, shower, love, and live life? I'm not looking to achieve or please. I just want it done right. I'm always combing over these areas in search of the best way, but it leaves me isolated from others. The gift I bring to the chaotic areas of my life can hinder my ability to love others. Imagine a person who in his heart wants to help and serve and thinks he knows how you should change to improve your life, and he constantly shares that with you. You can imagine how annoying that is, and you can quickly see how it creates a void between me and those around me. The void grows because there's no relational humility. Reformers can't see how we need the people we're reforming, and it leads us to the delusion that we are autonomous. Community rebels against this lie of isolation.

When our community moved to the Philippines, I took my kids into the slums, ate the food, drank the water, played basketball, set up medical cooperatives, and held Bible studies. However, during this time away, my college ministry in Tampa was experiencing a season of harsh criticism and division within the student leadership, and it was only intensified by some poor leadership choices that I made. On a weekly, almost daily basis, I received critical e-mails and confrontational conversations that told me how I failed, hurt, or angered others. Being a 1, each failure that got pointed out was piercing, and each conversation felt like another weight placed on me. It felt like relentless blows to my heart that I could hardly endure, but I kept going even though I felt extremely worn down. I found myself carrying my past mistakes as an enormous burden into a cross-cultural situation where mistakes were a daily occurrence. It was too much for me to bear. I felt overwhelmed with uncertainty and unable to make any choices because they all led me to more mistakes and imperfection. What do you do when every choice can bring about another series of accusations?

Those feelings led me into my deepest depression. Where was God? Why did he seem so distant? Where was his voice in my life? All I wanted was to escape. That was when my propane tank (so to speak) caught fire, and it was there, in my community, that Jesus healed me. It was the best and worst night of my life. In our hot, sticky living room during our community meeting, my mask came off. I was confronted about being superior and independent. I was overcome with the fear of being left alone because I was not worthy or good enough for these relationships. I was deeply flawed, a minister who should not be allowed to do ministry. I couldn't contain myself. I couldn't defend myself. All I could do was cry. But what happened next was the most healing moment of my life. My community stood around me and loved me—the imperfect me. We moved to our prayer room, and I was prayed for by my community to be filled with God's love. Together, we wept and cried out to God. His Spirit and their loving faith took away all the weight of the criticisms and my failures. I thought I could work hard enough to solve anything, but I could not. I thought I could make myself feel God's love, but I was left empty. I didn't deserve the friendships, love, and laughter of a community, but I had it. I needed them to carry my burdens and lift me up to the Father, and that is what they did.

Carrying each other's burdens is not an uncommon experience in community. We have faced many tragedies involving our families and each other over the years. Together, we've experienced heart-wrenching stuff that typically destroys the lives of families. We've walked with each other, loved each other, and carried each other's burdens, and in the middle of all the pain of our lives and ministry we've laughed. If Jason didn't get up at some point in a meeting and begin dancing with the most awful rhythm, just to make us laugh, then we knew something was wrong. Of course, we've carried some jokes way too far, but that is okay too; there is a rich joy that exists between us. We are not out of our minds. We are sober about the pain of this world, yet when we are together Jesus draws joy from within us.

Community Has Kept Me Guessing

I enjoy working out, and I think there are some lessons to learn from it. It keeps me calm and helps discipline my life. In physical training, there is a theory that your body quickly responds to any exercise routine but then plateaus, which makes it difficult to see any additional improvement. To continue growth, trainers instruct you to "confuse your muscles" so that your body cannot anticipate the routine. Muscle confusion keeps your body guessing and allows you to see continual improvement.

In the same way as we pursue Jesus and grow in our character we can hit plateaus. Sometimes we believe the lie that we've arrived or have achieved so much. It's true: God has shaped us tremendously. But we have not arrived yet. Sometimes our routines that were once radically stimulating spiritually start lacking the intrigue, adventure, and passion we once experienced. Fasting was like this in my life. Each time I fasted, it was a great stepping stone in my life. However, after a few years it became routine, and I needed to be careful it didn't become a simple religious act without a function. If I want to continue to know Jesus more and be challenged to grow, then I need something to keep me guessing.

Community requires me to keep moving and be alert. You never know what's going to happen each week. Someone might have a word of encouragement, a crisis, or a challenge to bring. Everyone brings his or her unique situation and stimulates thought and passion for Jesus and His kingdom. When I come to our weekly meeting understanding I need these people and I expect Jesus to pour into my life through them, I see how Monica's relentless questions come from an underlying care and concern for peace in others. I can see how Crystal's creativity and different perspective keeps me from being too focused, and Joann's infectious joy for coffee, cookies, or really any snack teaches me the joy of living in the moment. In the midst of jokes and the tragedies in our lives, these lessons are continually repeated every time we're together.

Community has never allowed me to get too comfortable. In community, I'm too exposed and out there for people to see. I can fake it to those outside but not these people. They've seen me at my best and worst, and they know the entire spectrum of who Jesus has made me to be. This doesn't mean I spend every night exposing every thought and secret lust of my heart to everyone. It simply means my mask of insecurity doesn't last long in a community that really knows me.

Community and Mystery

Sometimes the most difficult part of any exercise routine is just getting started. In the same way, our community had some of our hardest times in the beginning as we were getting to know each other. As we interacted with each other and wondered what those actions meant, we found plenty of confusion, heartache, anger, and conflict. There was no way around it. Occasionally, the conflict came from an ignorance of the people around us, but it was all pretty messy.

We looked for different ways to understand each other better. When we discovered our enneagram types, we were able to see how each individual was contributing to the community and how our fears and motivations sometimes caused us to say things and act in peculiar ways. With a commitment to our community and a fresh understanding of each other, we were able to move toward submitting to each other out of trust.

I don't like surprises. I like to anticipate what needs there are and then offer solutions. A difficult reality for a perfectionist in community is that true needs and solutions are sometimes a mystery to us. I have to be cautious because sometimes the things I wish to change in others are actually the exact ways they are needed in the community. We can attempt to anticipate how someone's personality might be useful for a specific situation, but God likes to change things up. As we live in this mystery, we submit to each other, trusting that person will be used by Jesus to be the solution to our needs. It is God's gift to us that these moments remain a mystery. Otherwise, our need for community would be reduced into a need for just a counselor or a motivator, not the actual person. God's gift in real community is giving us the heartbeat that says, "I need you. I don't know how exactly. All I know is I need you."

Our worlds don't slow down, and often relationships suffer because they become secondary to social networks, promotions, and our children's sports leagues. The commitment to community is a burden, but it's a light burden like carrying a blanket for warmth in the winter. Sometimes it seems to take up too much space, and you think of all the things in your closet you could fit if you didn't have it. Then, when the cold weather comes you don't dream of all the extra storage that blanket took up.

As a reformer, it hasn't been easy to engage in community and realize my need for others, but to know that people will be with me, will love me, and will not leave me because of my imperfections is a freedom I've never known anywhere else.

5

TYPE TWO:
The Helper/Healer
Jennifer Bartlett

The Caring, Interpersonal Type:
Demonstrative, Generous, People-Pleasing, and Possessive

When you think of Disneyland, you probably think of Mickey Mouse. For me, Disneyland was the first time I recognized the role reversal of my mother and I. I was 10 years old. My father took my two younger brothers on Splash Mountain while my mother and I shopped. She had a progressive mentally and physically debilitating disease and was in a wheelchair by this time. As we went from store to store, we lost track of time, and after 2 hours we realized we had no idea how to get back. Crowds of people pushed up against us, and I fought to push my mother against the constant stream of people. I began to feel afraid. She repeatedly asked me how much farther it was to get back to our family, and each time there was an increasing amount of fear and anxiety in her voice. I kept repeating to her, "I don't know, Mom. I don't know how to get back." Finally, I thought she would know what to do, so I asked her. She answered in an angry tone, "I don't know, but you had better get me back to your father right now." In that moment, I realized I was responsible to get us back, and somehow I did.

I burst into tears at the sight of my father because I had been so afraid and overwhelmed. It was a relief when I saw him because I knew I was no longer responsible. Later, my father told me that I rose to the occasion when they had needed me most. He and my mother hugged me and told me how much they loved me. I began to understand that to be needed was to be loved. Six years later there was no relief from the responsibility of being needed since my father was gone, my mother was fully dependent both physically and mentally, and I found myself in charge of her and my brothers. Because my father no longer needed us, I believed he didn't love us. Until community, I completely believed that to be needed was the only way to be loved.

Community Is Being Loved, but Not Needed

Community has been a journey to being loved and not needed. My brokenness was challenged by eight people who did not really need me but chose to love me for some other reason. They did not love the flawless person I tried so hard to project but the real me who was needy, slightly socially awkward, and prideful. It has been a place of struggle to be known and not needed. It has been a place where I have grown in my relationship with Jesus. It has taught me about choosing to love people in the fullness of who they are, including their strengths and weaknesses.

To my surprise, the people in my community want me around. They tell me so all the time. If I am missing, they notice. They find me and tell me I am missed. They don't require me to earn it. They just want me to be with them. My whole life I have been surrounded by people in need. The common thread has been meeting those needs and getting my sense of worth from being able to. At 16 years old, I would come home from school to the needs of my mom and brothers as soon as I entered the door, and I would meet them. I would feel capable and valued. I believed my value was tied to meeting everyone's needs.

This ideology left out the biblical truth of having worth because God made me in his image and chose me. Living in a community of people who want me not for what I can do for them but for who I am is the way Jesus continues to reveal my true value. As a nurse, I meet needs all day. But the two most profound parts of my day are when I leave and when I come home. Often when I am about to leave, Monica or Joann will say, "Don't leave!" They don't say it because they need me to do something for them but because they love me. When I return home they say, "We missed you," and it's not because they missed what I could do for them but because they love me. Each time I leave and come home, I am reminded by God that it is better to be loved out of desire than need. This is true for the whole community as well. When someone is absent, there is a longing for that person to be with us—not because we need them but because we long for who they are.

Community Exposes Pride

The more radical truth is that my community has firsthand knowledge of my many flaws, and they still want me. This has been the greatest area of healing. They love me through my failures. They don't leave because I am flawed. It is one of the greatest gifts I receive from community. This is not only true for me, but for each of us. We are all wanted by one another. We have all had our sins and weaknesses exposed, and we still choose to love one another.

Being wanted is wonderful, but it creates tension in my life because I've always found my identity in being needed. That tension has created major struggles with my pride and seeing my uniqueness. The day I got my mother and me back to our family at Disneyland was also the beginning of my friendship with pride. As I have examined that event (and others like it) I think I began to believe that I was better than my mother because I was stronger than her. I could do what she could not. This became true for everyone whose need I could meet when they were too weak to meet their own. When my dad left, I was in charge of my family, and I believed I was better than all of them. They rarely challenged me when I was wrong, perhaps because they needed me. I also convinced myself I could meet my own needs.

In a twist of wonderful irony, my invitation into community came out of my need for a place to live to return to school in Tampa. That was the beginning of my discovery that my pride is like an enemy masquerading as a friend. Conflict with my true friends has been a light revealing my pride as the real enemy. Having conflict means you are exposed in some way. I held on tightly to my pride and the false image in my mind that I was better than I really was. Everyone could see my sin except me. It would take hours of conflict for me to see it and admit I was wrong. Since my community didn't need me to do something for them, they could be honest with me about my sins, and because I was not needed by them I could not claim to be better than them.

I began to feel insecure in my relationships with them. With every conflict, every failure, every weakness exposed, I couldn't understand how people who saw all of these sins and failures could still love me. Why would they stay? My family saw my weaknesses and failures, but because they needed me they stayed. My dad saw my weaknesses and failures, but he didn't need me and left. My understanding of what real love is has come from my community, who does not need me and who sees the reality of who I am in all my sin yet still chooses to stay. If all people know about me is a false image of who I am, then I am not really loved. My community helped me remove the mask I wore, saw my true face, and declared, "This is who we choose to love."

Embarrassingly, there is still a remnant of brokenness in me that wants to be needed and believes I am better than others. It empowers my pride, and I cling to it. I am like the man in the book of James who looks at his reflection in the mirror but goes away and forgets what he looks like. My community lovingly holds up the mirror again, and I return to the place of humility that I'm a sinner and I cannot earn my place. Jesus reminds me that I don't have to be perfect or needed to be loved. He teaches me this is true for others. I don't need my community the same way I used to. I am free to love them as they have loved me because I choose to. Everyone in my community has been exposed and confronted with his or her sin. We have all had to be honest with one another, and we have all committed to staying and loving one another.

Community and the Search for Uniqueness

The other major struggle I have wrestled with is not feeling unique within my community. Being needed gave me the feeling of being unique. When I did not feel unique, I became envious of people and their strengths. But I have learned to rely on Jesus to define who I am. When I begin to equate being unique with what I can do, my community presses me to find my identity in Jesus and not in what I can do. Over time I have found more of my identity in him. I realize now that I am unique but that it is not because of what I do but because of who I am. I have also learned to combat my envy with appreciation and celebration for people and their uniqueness. When I see their uniqueness without envy I often see how I am different from them. The contrast builds us both up. I have come to learn that it is important to retain our uniqueness and not become clones of one another and that loving each other in our strengths is as important as loving each other in our weaknesses.

I have a deeper relationship with Jesus because I live in community. I have learned that God loves us because he chooses to. There is nothing that we can do to earn his love. From childhood, I operated under the false impression that you can earn someone's love by meeting his or her needs, and you lose love when you sin. Jesus crushed those lies with the tangible love I receive in community—love that I have not been able to earn by meeting their needs, that I have not been able to lose through my sins. I have been able not only to receive this love but also to demonstrate it to people in my community, ministry, and family.

John wrote, "We love because he first loved us," and my life is a portrait of that truth. (1 John 4:19) I have been made a rich woman by the love of Jesus and my community. I don't think I could have experienced this level of understanding of the Father's love, or love people as deeply as I do now, outside of community. I have also begun to learn the application of what Paul says: "Do nothing out of selfish ambition or vain conceit but in humility consider others better than yourselves."(Philippians 2:3) I still sometimes meet people's needs out of vanity and pride; I still struggle with this cancer in my soul. But Jesus offers the treatment of humility by placing me with people who have shown me I am not better and that I am often the weak person in need. My eyes have been opened to see how I have been fighting for the enemy of pride against my truest friend Jesus. I have begun to switch sides because of community by assuming I am probably wrong in a conflict. I have begun to see others, even those who need me, as better than me because I now see how broken I am.

Community has shown me it is radically better to be wanted than to be needed. As I have gained resources of my own, I have come to a place where I do not need my community as I had once before. I can freely choose to leave or stay, but I stay because I love them. I have lived in community for 10 years now, and I know and am known by these people. They are my closest friends, and I cannot imagine my life without them. They are one of the greatest gifts I have received from Jesus.

The next chapter of my life has been a call to adopt an orphan, and as I write this, that process is under way. The whole community is excited about the prospect of a new addition to our home. As I have been adopted into the family of God, I have had the increasing desire to adopt someone who does not know what it means to be wanted. My community has been a source of encouragement for me throughout this process. They are as committed to my future child as I am. I can't wait for my kid to be wanted and loved by me, by my community, and most importantly by Jesus. My prayer is for the next 10 years of my life to be a pouring out of the love I have received from Jesus through my community over the last 10 years.

6
TYPE THREE:
The Achiever
Jason Thompson

The Success-Oriented, Pragmatic Type:
Adaptive, Excelling, Driven, and Image-Conscious

I am a dreamer. I like grand ideas. Couple that with an overinflated need to achieve, and you have the makings of a longing to live a life on the edge. After a few years of wandering spiritually, my heart came to rest in Jesus. I began following Jesus at the age of 21. What struck me about Jesus was how he lived a life that was radical. I was someone who liked to be on the edge, and as I have followed Jesus I have discovered that he is found on the edge of things. Those edges for me have been serving and preaching the gospel to college students, living in the inner city of Tampa for many years, learning from urban church planters in the slums of Manila, and most recently relocating my family to plant churches in Germany. These are some of the edges where I have discovered Jesus. Yet the edge that has most shaped me as his follower has been the life I have lived with others for over a decade in intentional community.

The idea of living in intentional community was put before me in spring 1997. I was newly married, and the possibility of living with Brian and Monica (plus some college students) in the same house in the inner city of Tampa stirred my heart. As I read the gospels, I discovered that Jesus lived the kind of life that was deeply involved with others. He traveled with them, shared meals with them, wept with them, and served with them. He was a radical but not a loner. He called others into sharing life together with him. His invitation to this kind of life was most often simple.

For me, his invitation came through a friend. I can still remember sitting at our little table in a small apartment with my wife, Katy, and my friend, Brian, as we talked about what it would be like for our families to live together, sharing all we had in one of the harshest neighborhoods of Tampa. At the time, we were not the closest of friends. We knew each other on the surface from being a part of a campus ministry together, but knowing each other to start living in community did not matter to me. The proposal to live with others in a way that somehow reflected the life I imagined Jesus shared with his disciples was too important to pass up. I had no idea all that I was saying yes to, much like many of the choices I have made to follow Jesus, but I did know it was his heart and direction for me and that was enough.

For many years, my community, this radical band of Jesus' people, has been my closest friends. Each of them has been my teachers, confidants, encouragers and challengers. They have taught me more by the choices they have made to follow Jesus day in and day out than I could place value on. Together, we have walked to the edges with Jesus.

Community and the Drive to Succeed

Our first night in community is forever burned in my memory. Most communities go through a honeymoon phase; unfortunately, it lasted only a few hours for me. Appearances sometimes get the best of me, and it seems that from day one Jesus would not have that dictating my life in community. I was to be exposed quickly. Our first night living together was just after taking a short-term missions trip to Haiti. Toward the end of the trip, I managed to get sick in a way that led me to use the bathroom far more often than I would have liked. Imagine your stomach rumbling, panic setting in, and then sprinting to the nearest toilet. Our first night under the same roof was met with my announcement to all in my new community of how sick I was and my desperate need for first priority in the bathroom. Everyone cracked up laughing. Forget any effort at trying to cover things up, as hard as I tried—and trust me, I tried. It is just that when you live in community you live exposed. Everyone sees, hears, smells, and knows your weaknesses. Why try to hide? It is impossible.

Community that is authentic won't allow for hiding. No community can survive apart from being built and rallied around love for one another, weaknesses and all. Jesus himself gathered a community of 12 who, intentionally or not, wore their weaknesses on their sleeves and were loved in spite of it. From brothers who were hot-tempered to those who were impulsive, cheats, and doubters, Jesus included and exposed them all.

Community without exposure is not true community. I know that it sounds beyond belief to think that you could be loved in spite of your weaknesses, but it is true. It is risky and scary for those of us who want to maintain our masks, our appearances. However, it is the one thing that we most need, and it may be the one thing that has been most difficult for me in community. The biggest struggle for me in life has been trying to prove why people should love me. I work hard. I play hard. I am an achiever. Even in community I have strived to be the "best" community member. Initially, I was always asking myself the question, "Is everyone cool with me? Have I shared what is happening in my life? Have I selflessly helped someone else with a household task or a need that was not my responsibility? Have I asked others how they are doing?" Of course all of these are good things, but when your motivations are blurred with love for others and personal image management, it can be taxing.

It has been my struggle to be loved for who I am, not what I do or what I offer. The problem was I did not want them to love me in any way that was real. I did not want them to do anything for me. I wanted them to tell me how great I was. I wanted them to tell me what I had achieved for them. That way I felt loved and valued. I did not want to be loved in spite of my weaknesses. Then I would not have achieved anything. I struggled with wanting to be loved for my merits. That way I could control why people love me.

Life in community has taken this charade and crushed it. I can remember one of many times this has happened. It came in such a small way (as deep lessons often do)—sitting around with my community and talking about dishes. You see, I was the king of dishwashing in our community. No dirty dish, whether it was mine or someone else's, had a chance in my presence. It was a house joke. The job no one else wanted to do, I did the best. One evening, the motivation for being the dish guy was called into question. I was so offended and hurt. There was an insinuation that my dishwashing benevolence was the fruit of wanting the affirmation of others and not always about serving them. I was exposed. Perhaps it was not always true, but more often than not I gained so much self-value and identity from the appreciative comments or simply knowing that I was the ace of the community that I could not distinguish a desire to serve from my own need to demonstrate my competence as a member of the community. My world came undone.

It was not just doing the dishes that exposed me; it was so much more. It was an unhealthy work ethic, overextended schedule, and the tyranny of saying yes to everything and every person. It was the gift of community that opened my eyes to the chains that I dragged around unaware. Community moved me toward being honest with myself, something I greatly needed though often did not want. That has been my struggle, maintaining an image of importance and achievement versus being honest and self-aware.

Community and Clarity

We achievers are so busy accomplishing that we see and understand very little about what is taking place in our hearts. Perhaps what is most frightening for those with the same bent as me is that we don't see in ourselves what others can see as plainly. I believe it is because of this struggle that Jesus has placed me in an intentional community. He placed me in community to teach me that he does not love me for what I achieve.

He has placed me in a community to remind me that I am loved just because he chooses to love me. I am grateful for that lesson even though I still struggle to accept it. But it is better to struggle with people who love you in spite of your struggle. That is authentic and intentional community.

I think if I was asked why I have lived with other families and friends for so long I would say that it is because they do not love me for what I offer but rather for who I am. It is in being loved in this way that has sustained me. They have shown me the love of Jesus in a manner that is beyond expectation. Perhaps that may be the greater reason for living in community: it has brought me closer to people and in turn has brought me closer to Jesus and his leading in my life. There is no way that I would be in the place I am today apart from my community. Can you imagine being able to sit around on a Sunday evening sharing a problem or challenge that you are facing and to have eight other people committed to Jesus who are willing to speak into you and help discern God's wisdom in addressing that problem for you and with you?

In my community, I have a band of Jesus followers who bear my burdens and concerns as their own. It is not just love in words; it is love in considering the needs of others. They can see situations objectively and speak into them when I am deep in the forest of the problem.

Just recently, my wife and I felt Jesus calling us to be a part of planting a community of churches beginning in Hamburg, Germany. The task of discerning that calling alone seemed daunting. But in community that was not something we had to venture into alone. My wife and I talked, prayed, and shared with one another our thoughts, dreams, and concerns of going to Germany. We shared with the community what we were thinking. Then, in our effort to follow the example of the early church community in Antioch (Acts 13), the community agreed to devote a season of fasting and prayer to discerning Jesus' call for us to move to Hamburg. My wife and I went on a trip to pray and seek the Lord together, while knowing that our community at home was praying with us. Upon our return, we shared with all of them that we felt the Lord could be saying we should go. The community affirmed the decision for us to go in their own time of prayer, which I am sure will give us confidence that will sustain us in the future.

Community as Shared Pain

Living in community is a consistent reminder of Jesus' goodness and mercy. In winter 1999, my sister, Kimberly, was diagnosed with lymphatic cancer. The news was devastating. Katy and I drove to be with her and care for her as she battled cancer. After much discussion with our family, we decided it was best for Kimberly to come live with our community. She would be among a family of Jesus-centered people who could help care for her. Overnight, Kimberly went from having two caretakers—Katy and me—to a houseful of adults who all shared in loving and serving her. It was amazing. Kimberly experienced the love of Jesus in a powerful way, and she also committed her life to Jesus. After months of treatment and care I wish I could say Kimberly's health improved. Unfortunately, her health deteriorated under all the treatment, and she died in early December 1999. I was undone. I had not known pain and suffering like that ever before. In spite of all that, Jesus provided in my community a harbor of joy and solace in the midst of my mourning. I did not have to walk through that experience alone. They cried with me and struggled to move on with me. Community became even more real for me when my friends shared my tears.

Everyone in our community has a story of walking through tremendous struggle with us by their side. Our community is big enough that someone is always struggling with something important. Life in community has been my catalyst to a deeper life of following Jesus. It has been in community that I have known more deeply the heart of Jesus toward me and others, as daily the concerns and needs of others whether big or small are always before me. That is not to say it is taxing; rather, it is a reminder to me that I am not the center of the universe and that there are times more often than not where the needs of others are more important than my own. It is difficult to get upset or frustrated over something simple or mundane in your own life when someone in the community is really struggling. In that moment, their need is greater, so that need comes first.

Interestingly enough, a secret to life in community is this: If I put the needs of others before my own needs and live in a community that does the same, then my needs are taken care of because my community is looking to my needs as I look to meet theirs. It is truly the wisdom of Jesus. This is one lesson that has brought me closer to Jesus. He has used community to take care of me, to correct me, to encourage me, to remind me. I don't have to do all those things myself. And he has used community to force me to get over myself.

Community and Weakness

A great and simple example of this has been in our work at home repair. I am the most inept home repair person in our community and, quite possibly, the world. Don't get me wrong: I try. And the achiever in me dies a little more at each attempt because I rarely come out of a project with a sense of the satisfaction of a job well done. Brian and Jeremy, on the other hand, are quite handy. So imagine for years of my life working with those guys on home repair projects. You name it, we have done it, or, better put, they have done it. I honestly offer very little help. At times I have wished I had more to offer and have been frustrated by my incompetence, but today I am okay with it. I don't have to know everything. I don't have to be competent at everything. What is interesting is that in the midst of my inability to provide for home repair "know-how" I have discovered that there are other needs to be met on house workdays.

Sometimes the need is levity or a conversation about something happening that week or a challenge in ministry. That I can offer. Is it hammer and nails or measuring things accurately? Not from me. But rather it is something else that is needed. Of course, I gain much from these experiences as well. I learn from Brian and Jeremy not only about 2-by-4's but also about growing in ministry, what it means to be a man after God's heart, and how to serve as a leader in the kingdom. Jesus knows my need for such lessons and has given me two good friends to teach me that. Work projects are so often not about the task at hand but about something much deeper that affects much more, and not being able to do the work kills me. The achiever in me dies, but the truth is that some of that needs to die. Jesus knows that, and he is working to form his character in me. His tool for this refining of my character has been community, so he gave me friends, more competent than I to teach me and to guide me, to encourage me and to challenge me. Hopefully in other ways I have done the same for them. I am so blessed and thankful that Jesus does that. Would I have learned any of this apart from community? Maybe or maybe not. But community has guaranteed that I will.

When I said yes to Jesus years ago it was done with the anticipation of an adventurous, radical life. I was sure that Jesus had called me to himself and to follow him on the edges. The truth is there is no way I could have ever lived the radical life I longed for alone. Jesus gave me a community to form his character in me and to push me to live on the edge. Community has been Jesus' means of grace and challenge in my life. It has prompted me to lay down my desire to be loved for my merits. It has offered me love that is without conditions. It has given me direction and hope in serving Jesus. It has been the means of God's work in my internal life. This community that started long ago as a band of strangers has become a family that is forever. We sit with Jesus, members of his family as those who, together, do the will of the Father. This life in intentional community is truly a life lived on the edge.

7
TYPE FOUR:
The Individualist/Artist
Crystal Haralambou

The Sensitive, Withdrawn Type:
Expressive, Dramatic, Self-Absorbed, and Temperamental

I have an old scrapbook that contains a weathered photo of me in the height of middle school. I was wearing denim-patterned overalls with a belt. My hair was big. The picture graciously captures some of who I still am. I was far from ordinary. I didn't blend in well. I had my own sense of style and worth. I lived outside the lines of what others expected of me. I was finding my footing and wanted to say, "Look at me, I'm original." I believe my motto back then was "Make the most interesting choices." I avoided conformity, resisted authority just enough, and fought hard to create and maintain a colorful life full of adventure, risk, and authenticity. This individuality has stuck with me, and life in community hasn't always been fluid. I'm still the one who would venture to wear the odd outfit. I still have big hair. I tend to be outspoken. I laugh hard or think deeply about things and only rarely can you find me on an average point along this spectrum.

So how do I survive in community? At first glance, someone might assume life in an intentional community would consume the artist, leaving little originality in the end. I have lived in community since 1998, and I can honestly say that it has enriched my life in ways I never expected. At times it feels complicated, but in the process of sharing your life, the artist is awakened. We are pressed to not only see the pain in the world, which tends to be more natural for the artist, but also to face the weaknesses in ourselves as well — a much harder feat at times.

Living in community often reveals what is hidden in our personality and requires truth to bring it into the light. Here, the artist learns far more about himself or herself, more than one would living alone. Despite all of the insecurities, the artist knows that their identity is continually evolving. In that evolution, community helps you understand the immediate impact your feelings, moods, and perspectives have on the people around you. You learn that self-authenticity is not more important than relationships.

Life in community cultivates humility for the artist, something that is rarely found in the artistic community at large. It grounds the individualist and a balance is achieved. Because opposites attract, the artist thrives in this environment in surprising ways. You feel loved without having to prove that you are worthy of it. In fact, you are often not worthy. Your weaknesses rise to the top for all to see, and you are loved despite those weaknesses. Likewise, a community that embraces an individualist is also stretched.

The artist has strengths that God has placed in us. In these strengths the artist also serves the whole of the community. We lean towards truth, see things differently, speak fearlessly, and even defend our perspective. (Consequently, we have to accept the fact that sometimes, we are wrong). We are uniquely made by God and our individuality is celebrated in community, among people who truly know us, sometimes better than we know ourselves.

Community and Acceptance

Protecting my flaws is high maintenance, but life in community levels the playing field. Here I discover that I'm not the only one with a mask on, and what's more, it is all right to take it off, to be myself, even if I am different.   I've come to the conclusion that living in community doesn't fix my problems—it reveals them. Personal facades get peeled back and discarded, illuminating multiple chins of sin, and muffin tops of failure, yet we still love each other. By sharing our lives, we're given the opportunity to strengthen one another. With prayer and submission to God, true transformation is possible.

It has taken me a long time to admit that I am flawed, but why? It's not like other people didn't notice all along. In community, truth reigns, and you reconcile with it at some point along the journey; only then can healing begin. The wonderful part is that you have people cheering you on when you face those giants — people with monsters of their own, who will also call upon your strength at some point. I have had others hold up a mirror to my flaws and defects I could never see for myself. The truth is sometimes painful, but it heals as it reveals a more authentic me. Shame doesn't retain its hold on you because you realize that everyone has something to hide and truth is liberating. We hold each other's hands, walk toward the crashing waves, and jump in. Somehow, the ugliness of life, the flabby knees and saggy parts, don't seem to matter in light of your inner beauty. Mingled with heartache and pain, one begins to live a more disciplined life, which ultimately leads to a greater sense of joy. The preoccupation with girdles, skinny scoops, or under bust waste cinchers disappears right along with the insecurities.

We are altogether overwhelmed and captivated by something much larger than our myopic view of ourselves. Our perspective is fixed on something that seems to have no beginning and no end. We tremble at its enormity, depth, and vastness. It beckons, cleanses, and frightens us. We rest in it, we are renewed by it, and we are dumbfounded when the seemingly impossible has become a reality. The individualist is humbled by the cleansing transformation that takes place in our lives when we find ourselves in community. We see the effects of transformation in the lives around us and it changes us. Though as an individualist, it is not always easy to see it from this angle.

Community and Disclosure

Life in community requires authenticity. Authenticity requires risk. As an individualist, a chasm exists between disclosure and secrecy. I longed to be true to my feelings, but initially I was only ready to step into community if I could create an image of someone I wanted to be. Individualists tend to feel both pain and joy more deeply. Early on, I was made aware of how these sensitivities affected the people around me. I could color a room with my hilarity or shut it down cold with my melancholy mood. As an individualist in community, changing felt impossible. I wanted to be who I was, true to my feelings without having the pressure of affecting others. I had a rough time knowing what and how much of myself to reveal. I would let my feelings get the best of me on confrontational nights, and I often said too much of the wrong thing or not enough of the right thing. This is the tension that the individualist deals with in community and perhaps in life. We want to be innately honest with ourselves, but self-authenticity cannot be traded for relationships unless you want to live in a world all by yourself.

I had to learn the hard way to pause and consider the other people involved, to care for them and acknowledge how my presence, actions, commitment or lack thereof was affecting them. It may sound elementary, but I had to learn to listen more carefully and truly esteem them more valuable than my emotions or myself. This can feel confusing for individualists, especially when we're working so hard to let our own guards down. While I've always admired people who are disconnected from their feelings and do what is right because it makes the most logical sense, I do not discount the importance of leaning on one's intuition. The hard lesson for the individualist to learn is that people are more important than one's feelings. Over the years, I learned to trust the perception of my community, especially when my own emotions have left me confused and stymied.

Ultimately, losing the mask sometimes means you hurt people's feelings in the wake of discovering your true self, which is why you constantly have to remind yourself that loving people takes precedence. When self-actualization does come, you're often surprised to find that you aren't the person you thought you were — you're actually better because you begin to reflect the image of God, who knows the real you and loves you just the same. Community reminds you that you were made in His image. To love is to know God. "Let us love one another, for love comes from God. Everyone who loves has been born of God and knows God. Whoever does not love does not know God, because God is love." (1 John 4:7-8)

Community and Envy

The root sin for the individualist is envy. For most people who do not have the artist's sensitivities, life's a beach. They are blissfully content with a day beneath the sun, casually enjoying light conversation and the company of others. For me, I am drawn by the mystery of what is beneath the surface.

Individualists love beauty and art. We believe in dreams and little keeps us from being spontaneous, imaginative or creative. We often get lost in memories of the past or daydreams about the future. Consequently, we miss the present moment completely. Individualists often have just enough dissatisfaction with their current world that they tragically long for something else and miss living in the here and now. When I am able to resist this and stay in the moment, I find such joy and truth, that I wonder how I could have been lured away in the first place. I can't tell you how many times I have dreamed of moving to a culturally rich city, doing innovative theater in a far corner of the world, or inventing a product that people never knew they needed. Clearly none of these things in and of themselves are bad. However when I'm not daydreaming, my life is rich with deep friendships, and shared experiences. Living in the present allows me to see that all of my needs are abundantly met. I belong to a hilarious group of best friends that creates a house culture longing to see Jesus glorified. These are good things that should be celebrated.

Community requires your presence, attention, and active participation. While I was absent from countless community gatherings, emotionally disconnected, or busying myself with my own needs, I sensed that I had traded beauty for daydreams and had edited myself out of laughter or tender dialogues with my truest friends. I was gasping for air in a world of "what ifs," sacrificing the blessings of living in the present.

The individualist has an ego. We want to feel special. We want to leave our footprint on the world. We don't want a casual afternoon with a friend, but rather some epic memory that we can point back to and relish over, even if the memory is embellished and far from accurate. We tend to be the people that stand out in a crowd. We take pride in being different and unique, but our ego rears its ugly head, and we want to be the center of attention. Fortunately, community reminds us this was not God's design.

As an individualist it is hard to discern what my heart actually craves and what is simply envy. The part of me that longs to be uniquely different constantly wrestles with the part of me that longs to fit in. It is tiring. Envy disguises herself. She is a funhouse mirror reflecting life disproportionately. In the dissatisfaction of the moment, envy robs the individualist of joy. The world tells us we should have achieved particular accomplishments by the time you turn 30. Community rejects that standard and reminds us to listen to God's plan. Unfortunately, individualists sometimes still long for what we do not have. Ironically, once we possess it, we often no longer want it. The terrible sacrifice is the present moment. Wishing and hoping I was in someone else's shoes is time wasted. Community reminds you of what is real.

Community as an Epic Story

Shakespeare once said, "All the world's a stage." From my acting perspective, I have come to understand that community removes the individualist from our self-proclaimed spotlight and puts us backstage out of sightlines. We raise the curtain on another because there is something beautiful about humility and bringing light and honor to others. We naturally want to feel special and stand out, but when we live in community, we accept metaphorical lenses. We view things a certain way, a communal way. We have to think of our fellow players and trust them. We consider others with the choices we make. Our timing, precision, or lack to show up affects them. Community demands that we trade in our monologues for a chance to be a part of an epic story. When everything in us longs for people to understand where we are coming from, for them to grasp our vision, we have to listen, step back, and give them the benefit of the doubt, even if it means abandoning our agenda.

Community is a collaboration directed by God. He is the playwright. He does the casting. He has the vision. Our job is to take direction. Together, we ask God what his will is. Then we listen. This may be the hardest thing for the individualist, because we constantly want to feel exceptional, successful, and self-sufficient. We want to be the star in a one-man show. God transforms us.   Through community, we highlight the strengths of others to make sure their story unfolds. With God's help, we have to change our perspective and think of others first. At the end of the show we applaud wildly, whistle nonstop, and shout "Encore!" for God, for the story he told, his craftsmanship, and not ourselves. Worship is for God. As Jennifer reminded us in quoting Paul, "Do nothing out of selfish ambition or vain conceit, but in humility consider others better than yourselves."

This is not to say that as an individualist you solely spend your life adding to other people's stories. In community, balance is achieved and the individualist embraces humility. The costumes come off, the guises are gone, and each person is seen for who he or she is, compared with who God intended that person to be.

Community and Balance

Community gives the individualist balance. Community grounds the individualist. It offers us mental and spiritual health. Community reminds the artist of his or her gifts and who God created them to be. The individualist has to be authentic and loving in their communication with others — and when we fail, the community will lovingly correct you. Likewise, the individualist blesses the community by introducing a different perspective. We are often sensitive to certain issues. The artist's eye often sees things that others do not. We boldly speak up, articulating what others may think but are too timid to say. In many ways, we act as a conscience to the community. This truth that we speak sometimes shakes people out of their doldrums. This feels powerful and scary at the same time.

Community and Resolution

Once when I was a kid, we spent a long day at a distant beach and a friend of the family lost her car keys. I scoured the water's edge looking for them. We all did. It was getting dark, and we needed to find those keys to get home. That's when I prayed, "God, please help us find those keys." No sooner had I finished saying, "Amen," were the keys washed up on shore. We were jumping and shouting for joy because God answered my prayer. Finding resolution sometimes feels like searching for those keys on a beach. Nonetheless, we were focused on finding them, and praying was essential to our success.

Conflict scares the individualist. We don't want to disappoint others. We feel guilty when we do. We don't take criticism easily, and we don't want our harmonious boat to be rocked. These are all hard realizations, but resolution is different; it is a gift. Community devoted to resolution and with the help of God can say, "I see you now for who you are, and yes, I do love you." It says, "I can see a future you that is better than this." It cries out in the middle of the impossible and asks God for help. Through conflict and resolution, the individualists have to see beyond themselves. When we do this, we see that there are others involved who also have feelings. We have to be objective and considerate and remember that the goal of correction in the context of community is resolution. The gift of resolution is love. One of the things I cherish most about my community is its commitment to resolution. If those keys were resolution, then my community wouldn't leave the beach without them. This makes our relationships long lasting because no matter what, we are committed to seeing resolution.

Community and Solitude

I fully enjoy my friendships in community. However, when everyone else saw eye to eye, my different way of thinking has left me lonely at times. When I speak truth and find myself isolated in my thinking with my friends coming from another angle, I have to trust that God will help us through it and that our commitment to find common ground will be met whether they convince me of their perspective or I persuade them of mine.

Overall, community has been truly hard and extremely wonderful at the same time. Both emotional and spiritual growing pains have occurred over the years, but I sometimes wonder what my life would have been like if I was left to jump those hurdles alone. There is a reward of deep friendship that comes through a commitment to honesty and resolution. My friends know me, and I know them. They make room for me to be unusual and extraordinary. They honor my peculiar way of thinking. They balance me out when my perception of others or myself is off. They love me as an individualist, uniquely made by God, and I love them for the way God has distinctly created them. They allow me to be artistically different. They support me in my creativity no matter how it is revealed, and they often listen to my perspective. They don't define me by my flaws. They notice them, and they love me anyway. They trust God is molding my life, and take joy that in some ways, when God so chooses, they get to be a part of it.

I sometimes still run for cover at the initial thought of someone seeing me for who I am, but it is less of a gut reaction these days. With friends who are willing to let down their guard, a culture is created where failure is only one part of the journey, and humility is honored with strength. I lean on them when I am unsure of what to reveal or how much or when I start believing that there is a mysterious life that is better than what God has given me now.

As long as I continue to live in community, my weaknesses will steadily rise to the surface. This is inevitable. My friends will persist in loving me, and, likewise, their failures will appear and reappear. We will challenge each other, listen, repent, and laugh about it later. They will bear with me, even when it is difficult. I believe that together we are better because their strengths complement my weaknesses. They model a way to humility, to learning, and to set a standard of grace for loving others and me. They help me to see my world with a kaleidoscope of complexity that embraces others. They will remind me that there is something very unique and creative about my present life. They are a spectrum of color to my life's canvas.

Community knit together like this embraces pain and presses toward joy. It is a diverse company of weaknesses that transforms into strengths after a group of people are committed to loving one another. Community takes all of us from our private sandcastles to the shared baptismal waters. No matter how humiliating, painful, or fearful the walk to the ocean, a cleansing of the soul and healing of the heart awaits — even for a unique individualist girl like me.

8

TYPE FIVE:
The Investigator
Katy Thompson

The Intense, Cerebral Type:
Perceptive, Innovative, Secretive, and Isolated

When I was asked to write my chapter for this book, I was not in favor of the idea. I thought the book was a great idea, but knowing my own limitations and fears I tend to use extreme caution with any new endeavor. Living in community was a lot like that for me. It was not something that came naturally for me, yet the experience helped me grow and brought me joy and belonging.

I don't think I realized what community was and what it would mean for my life when I said yes to moving in with Brian and Monica in the inner city of Tampa. My husband, Jason, and I had attended a large mission's conference in our first year of marriage. I was a semester away from finishing nursing school at the University of Florida and thought God might be calling me to spend time doing medical missions. At this conference, however, it was clear that God had other plans for us. Our more immediate prayer was about where we should move next for Jason to be able to finish up his own degree. Tampa was one of our choices. We were not sure what that meant for us and our heart to serve God on the mission field, but we made the decision to move to Tampa when I graduated.

Almost immediately after talking through that decision, Jason and I headed out to leave the conference center and ran into Brian. Knowing that he was doing ministry in Tampa, we were excited to see him and tell him of our decision. We had no idea that at that same time he had been praying about finding people to move into community with him and Monica as they felt God call them to move into the city. A few months later, he came to visit us and offered us an invitation to join him. We were honored to be asked and said yes.

Community and Trust

I am a very practical person, so Brian's explanation of how he thought living together in one house, sharing our resources, and thus freeing up extra resources to give to the poor really appealed to me. It made sense to share a mortgage, a washing machine, dinner, and so much more. Having grown up as the oldest of nine children, I was used to lots of people living together and sharing space. I soon found out that, although the sharing of "things" made sense, the sharing of myself was what was so much more difficult for me.

One of the most difficult things about living in community initially came from the attempt to explain to family what we were doing and why. We were asked questions like, "Why are you going to live with other people?" "Don't you want to own your own home for your own family?" or "What about when we want to visit?" which made it hard to feel supported and, at worst, caused my own questioning of the decision. Was this decision really a sign that we just weren't growing up and being mature? Was I really choosing between my family and my community?

What I learned through that difficult time of trying to explain what we had decided to do was that our life was going to be filled with decisions that would go against our culture and what made sense to those looking in from the outside. Jesus' own family never seemed to understand why he did what he did either. But in time our families realized that although they may not have understood all of the reasons we made these choices, they respected the fact that our lives were not going to be defined by the culture we lived in. Our choices were made based on how we felt God leading us to serve him and the world around us.

What became the bigger difficulty for me was figuring out who I was and how I could live in community and still be myself. For one thing, it was really difficult for me to completely open up to people I was just getting to know. Sharing my struggles and honest thoughts was hard. The first few years in community, I learned that trust was a big issue for me, both in terms of trusting God and trusting others. Could I trust these friends enough to share my fears? Could I trust them enough to take their collective advice in areas I needed to grow? Could I trust them with my insecurities and my sins? Would they really love me if they knew me that well? For a long time, I was quiet during times when we met together. I dreaded conflict, even if it didn't involve me. Although we had agreed that in love we would challenge each other to grow and help expose areas that needed to change, I often forgot the promise of love. Yet the only way to prove someone will love you through your deepest junk is to have those times where it seeps out and has to be faced head on. And over time I learned that my issues were not going to be enough to stop my friends from loving me. More than that, I would be able to work through them and even overcome some of them.

Perhaps the greater gift that my community gave me in helping me learn to trust them was helping me to trust God. The difficulty I had in trusting my friends was really a reflection of a deeper trust issue with God. I had a hard time trusting his promises to love me, forgive me, and always be with me. As my friends patiently prayed for me and waited for me to share and then showed that they still loved me, I was able to understand the love that God has for me and to begin to trust him with my life.

Although life in community was great for my marriage, it was a struggle in the beginning because Jason really embraced this new life of sharing everything and made such a huge effort to spend time with our community, always taking every opportunity to build relationships and really offering all he had to make it work. I, on the other hand, felt an internal struggle that caused some very external tension between us. I wrestled with feeling a need for more personal space and time to myself and wondering if that was okay in community. Unfortunately, instead of sharing that struggle with my community, I usually argued with Jason about it, which often brought an ugly picture of forcing him to choose between spending time with me and with our friends. Frequently, I avoided spending time with my friends because I thought I needed to prove to myself that I could have my own time and space.

In the end, God used those friends to help me understand how I am wired and to help me filter out the sins of pride and stubbornness while encouraging the unique ways God created me. Not that I have conquered those sins—which is why I will need community in my life as long as I am breathing! But now I know that it is okay to need personal time and space and that I am not hurting anyone's feelings by admitting it. What's more, as I learned these things about myself and felt free to be myself I found that I was able to allow my community into that "personal space" more and more, and I didn't have to be the one to protect that space because I had eight other friends making sure I was doing okay.

Because of my initial resistance to the way things were meant to be in our community, I missed out on being able to reap the benefits a lot sooner. Of course, the practical benefits were in place merely by circumstance. We shared a home, shared the responsibilities of cooking and cleaning (making it possible to have a nice dinner every night with your friends but having to cook only once a week), and when our son, Nathan, was born we even had a built-in set of friends for him. But the best part of living in community is having a group of people that are always on your side, always rooting for you, and always pushing you to be the person God wants you to be. Had I trusted this sooner, I would have found that my community was not in competition with my need for time alone or space to myself. It is actually possible to have both alone time and time spent with friends, and both are life-giving for me. It was when I withdrew, both physically and emotionally, that I pushed away the gift that my community was for me. My thought was that withdrawing was the only way to protect my need for privacy or my ability to make my own choices. It was in those times that I was usually very self-absorbed and distrustful of the love that they had for me. I know now that when I share my struggles with my friends or ask for help in making decisions, the result is more Godly and rooted in love.

One very real situation that revealed my community's love not just for me but for those who were important to me occurred several years ago when I discovered that my sister was trapped in a difficult situation. She lived in another state, and my first instinct was to go and rescue her. However, my community's collective cry for justice and protection enabled me to move forward, knowing that I was not alone in trying to help her. Everyone in the house adjusted their lives, rearranged living space, and made a room for her to move into our community to be loved on by not just me but also my whole community. Jason and I had essentially become parents to a teenager overnight, and more than ever we needed the support and love of our community. The great thing was that every member of my community took on the responsibility that would have otherwise been solely ours to carry. Times like that showed me how meaningful and important life in community was.

Community as Adventure

Looking back over the last 13 years of sharing life with this community, my absolute favorite time was our 9-month move to Manila. I think because after many years of having a common vision but separate paths, it was nice to be focused on the same thing for a season. Being able to share such a life-changing experience with my closest friends really helped me view our community as more of a family. Even our struggles were similar, like learning to sleep at night in a non-air-conditioned room when sweat dripped down your face. Or being challenged to be grateful for our little van into which we squeezed nine adults and 10 children to travel through the dangerously congested streets of Manila. Or feeling the same heartache when we met a family who lived in a slum home that looked more like a small section of our city dump than a place where children should grow up. Sharing the tears and joys and cultural blunders and inability to speak the language and new Filipino friendships bonded us in a way that was really special to me. I think that of all our shared life those 9 months are the ones we love to reminisce about the most—the moments we love to laugh about and relive.

I think the most interesting thing that I have come to realize since that experience in the Philippines is that I don't want to do any part of life without a community. I have come a long way, and the gift that this specific community has given me is the love for community in general. As I have grown closer to my friends in this community, I have been able to open up my mind to appreciate community in different forms and with different people, which I didn't think was possible before that trip. In fact, at the time of writing this book, Jason and I are planning to move to Germany to plant a church. Our community has been fully behind this decision, but even knowing that this would mean an end to the way we have shared life for so many years we knew that we didn't even want to consider going without having a new community to go with us. So we have a small team, and we are working on strengthening this new group, knowing that community brings adventure to life ad that trying to do God's work alone just isn't as good or as fun as doing it with a group of people whom you love and who love you.

Life in community has taught me many things and has shaped the person I am today. Without community, my life would probably be boring and not very effective in changing the world for Jesus. I am much too analytical, needing everything to make sense and be mapped out before I can make a decision. While there is benefit to that kind of mind, having a community to push me to take risks for Jesus without knowing all the reasons why and how it will work has allowed me to be part of something great that I never could have dreamed of doing on my own. Another drawback to having such a well thought out mind is that I tend to trust myself more than Jesus. If I can plan it all out then I can do it—in my own strength. That always leads to failure, because it is based on pride, and even the best thought-out plans are not as good as what Jesus has planned for me.

If you struggle like I do, my encouragement is to first admit that trust is difficult for you and then to let Jesus prove his love to you through the love of other people. If someone in your community struggles with opening up, have grace for them and remind them frequently that you love them. My community has helped me to trust Jesus, not just in letting him lead me but also in trusting that he loves me. By loving me through good times and bad, they have been a physical display of God's unconditional love for me.

9
TYPE SIX:
The Loyalist
Jessica Stephens

The Committed, Security-Oriented Type:
Engaging, Responsible, Anxious, and Suspicious

When I was a child, I pictured my future with all the things I thought I needed. I planned for a good job, gifted children, an amazing husband, a grand house, and a perfect church where everyone loved each other. After I graduated high school, I planned to live my "American Dream" and to become someone important in life. However, soon after I arrived at college, my childhood faith was challenged by the university culture I experienced. I met different people with different ideas. I learned things about Jesus that I had never heard before. I took trips overseas where I interacted with the poor, and I began to see the life of Jesus in a very different way. It was a life full of hardship, pain, and sacrifice, yet also profound joy. My love for Jesus was growing, and I desired for those around me to know him the same way. Yet I constantly struggled with my need for security. All of my childhood dreams gave me control and independence. I knew that life was scary, and it was my responsibility to find the security those plans offered. This all changed when I moved into community.

In community, I learned how to let go of my desire for predictability and comfort and to exchange that fear for a life of adventure and sacrifice for the kingdom of God. Community helped me to see Jesus in new ways, and it became much easier to overcome many of the fears I held onto. I could face my fear of rejection because I saw Jesus as the rejected one, and my fear of being taken advantage of was eased because I saw Jesus, the king of the universe, submitted willfully to the abuse and demands of those he loved.

Community and Facing Fear

I felt a growing call from God to live a life that was different, but I knew that for that to happen I had to let some of my dreams die first. I hated that fear because as a follower of Jesus I sincerely wanted him to govern and motivate my life. I wanted to be the quiet, courageous, confident ambassador for Jesus, but many times I was too fearful. I had to learn that I could not live a secure life and a sacrificial life at the same time.

I began my journey in community like many others: idealistic, optimistic, and naïve. I was so excited and honored I was asked to join a community that already consisted of people I admired and respected. I probably said yes because I was so honored, but I had no idea what I was committing to. And they didn't know what they were getting with me.

Immediately after moving in, I could feel the space I had built around myself shrinking. People were around all the time. When I arrived home from class or work, there was almost always someone home, and I had a roommate again. People weren't just around. They continued to try to get to know me. I remember Monica always asked me how my day was, what I had been up to, or about the purity of my dating relationship. Once, Brian refused to leave until I explained why I had been feeling down. I didn't know what to do because I thought growing up meant becoming independent. I could learn to share my physical space, but I really struggled to learn how to share my heart and life with so many people. My subconscious desire for independence and control was very strong, and community magnified so many of my fears. I was afraid if my community really got to know me they would decide they didn't like me. I was afraid that if they really saw my sin and the ugliness of my heart they would decide I wasn't worth it and gently push me away. The desire for independence and control contradicted the idea of community. I wanted to feel secure in myself while they were pushing me to trust Jesus and to allow him to work through them to give me the security I was searching for.

As the community grew closer, our lives overlapped, and we found ourselves involved in more conflict. With each conflict, there were more opportunities to build trust and more opportunities for me to fail. I wanted to follow Jesus more than anything. I wanted to make the right decisions and to lead a sacrificial kingdom life. So I would say the right things, but my actions were not consistent with my words. There was no place to run—no place to pretend or project the false image of myself. People were getting to know the real me. There was no image to protect and maintain, and those were the times I realized what a gift community was for me. Everyone was so gracious and patient with me. They knew me the best and still loved me the most. There was a reflection of Jesus in each of the people in my community. They helped me to remember him, know him, and trust him more deeply because of the ways they are like him.

Community and Marriage

Jeremy and I were both single when we moved into our community. After about a year, we got married and chose to stay in the same house. It was a strange and difficult transition for me to go from sleeping in a bedroom with my roommate to sharing a room with my husband. I tried to act like I was so mature, but there were still a lot of awkward moments for me. In the same way I had my childhood dreams of what my life would look like, I also had very clear expectations of what I thought my marriage should look like. I thought Jeremy would care for me passionately, love me perfectly, and always want to be with me. But Jeremy had given his life to Jesus and his mission, and that didn't leave as much time for me as I had expected. I felt that my expectations were not being met and that it was his fault for not loving like he was supposed to. I immediately blamed him for my lack of security. I began to doubt that he really loved me. If he did, why did he want to love and serve others and not just me? Even though our community gently tried to remind me of this, I was stubborn. I interpreted their attempts to love me as not understanding me or being demanding when I was already feeling overwhelmed.

I never considered that maybe my expectations were too high and unrealistic. I forgot Jeremy belonged to God, not to me, and that just because we were married now didn't mean I would become the center of his life. I expected Jeremy to fill me like only God can. I wanted to control him and expected that to result in the security I longed for.

Jeremy and I have four kids now, and I continue to find my life much less self-focused and more complex. As a mother, I am not just seeking the Lord's will for my life or considering my own interests. I am constantly questioning the things that positively and negatively affect my children. My list of fears has been multiplied by four.

Sometimes I feel the conflict between the call of a sacrificial life and my motherly instincts. I want to live the kind of life that Jesus talks about where his followers leave behind everything, including family, houses, and livelihoods, for the sake of following after him and his kingdom's sake—where nothing matters except Jesus and his purpose. But are the sacrifices I make good for my kids too? Is there such a thing as too much sacrifice? I struggle with raising my children to live a sacrificial life in a culture that tells them to enjoy every indulgence. Ultimately, I fear ruining my kids, but even this is another opportunity for our community to show support and understanding.

During our time in the Philippines, I was able to experience life in community with kids. There were so many joys, blessings, and real benefits to this. There was always a willing hand to hold a baby when I needed to do something else or just needed a break. There was a freedom I experienced by sharing daily chores and cooking duties. As a mother of young children, I found such comfort and security in the moments of question and doubt with my community around me. I would look at my little boys' sweaty heads and heat rash, and I longed to ease their discomfort. Sometimes I wondered if I was placing them in danger by taking them into the slums, but I would look around and see the other parents in our community doing the same things and making similar sacrifices. It was so much easier to sacrifice and continue following after Jesus. Sacrifice can feel lonely, but living together makes it easier to see the joy Jesus promises in our sacrifice.

Community and Being Known

Our community laughs a lot. Sometimes it's as simple as a misspoken word that can become the joke of the night, the month, or even forever. Some of our jokes might get old, but it's actually one of things I appreciate most about our community. Things are not easily forgotten. This includes jokes and tragedies we've shared. There is a special kind of trust that is preserved in our community by not forgetting.

I crave that kind of intimacy. I remember a specific conversation between Jeremy and me. Our relationship was fairly new but serious enough that we talked about our long-term future together. We were on a road trip, and we were talking and dreaming about our future together. He told me a story about a childhood memory he had of cold mornings when his dad would get up early, go outside, and start his mom's car so that it would be warm by the time she was ready to leave. He said he admired his dad for that kind of servant-type love and hoped someday to treat me with the same love and service. I think I still remember that small conversation because of how it made me feel. It struck a longing so deep inside of me the memory is still with me today. I probably couldn't have even verbalized it then, but I can still remember the feeling. Could it be that someone would know me on such an intimate level and still like me enough to thoughtfully serve and respect me?

God, as only he can do, fills our inner longing to be known. I am amazed that in all of his splendor and glory God could desire to be known by us and to know him. In my relationship with Jesus I am often going back to that place of worship and awe understanding that he knows me. There is such a sweet place of intimacy and relationship between us when I am slightly able to comprehend him knowing me and loving me. "You have searched me, Lord, and you know me." (Ps. 139:1)

In my experience, good community is an example of our relationship with God. Jesus knows the real me in my state of depravity and still loves me with a deeper love than I've ever known. In the same way, the people in my community have been like that to me. They know the real me and love me still. We've been through it together, lived through it together, talked through it together, and reconciled together. And we remember it together. Because we remember, trust has been forged and maintained. I was reluctant (and still am at times) to share myself because that fear of rejection was such a deep part of who I was. But I know the trust that has been built runs deeper than my fears. We really know each other, not just at our best or what we want to be known for. And maybe that is really the only way to know someone.

10
TYPE SEVEN:
The Enthusiast
Joann Macabante

The Busy, Fun-Loving Type:
Spontaneous, Versatile, Distractible, and Scattered

I am a 7. The enneagram describes this personality type to be the life of the party because we are fun, energetic, and outgoing. We are adventure-seeking people who love to eat, drink, and be merry. Enthusiasts can tend to give in to gluttony because we don't know when to say no, and we are prone to addiction because we can overdo it. We are tempted to always be happy and to resist and avoid pain. We can often fall into depression and denial because of our refusal to accept hard things about ourselves. Without a doubt, that's me. While I enjoy hearing the good things about my personality, it is sobering and painful to learn the dark things that are also a part of me.

The night we discovered our unique personality types, there was a mixture of awe and sobriety in the room as we talked and agreed with the stuff that was true of us. Community has been a collection of memories like that night. At times, I felt skeptical, puzzled, surprised, and inspired. Looking back, I did not know living in community would redefine my entire life. I pursued Jesus with my whole life, and living that way with these people transformed the way I saw the world, myself, and ultimately my love for God. For me, community has been a journey home. Instead of chasing the next big thing, I found a place to grow roots and to go deeper in relationships, and in the process I found complete fulfillment and happiness.

Community as Home

For as long as I can remember, I have lived my life in the moment and rarely made long-term plans. I thought that was silly and unnecessary. If I had an idea or direction, I went for it. I was not an ambitious person, and I really thought the only thing I needed to fulfill my life was happiness. I loved taking those moments in, and I did my best to make it better, more enjoyable, and more memorable for those around me. I sought to indulge in life's buffet of pleasures and exciting experiences, and my simple outlook enabled me to have as much fun as I possibly could. While I tried to feel good at all times, this mentality gave me a hunger to always look for something bigger, better, and exciting and hardly kept me grounded. Rather than relying on facts and truth, I relied on my feelings to get me through tough times. Keeping my commitments wasn't a reason to stick around since I believed leaving would solve my problems or at best would make me feel better. I gave in to the idea that moving and starting all over in a new place would cause my problems to magically disappear. It was sad to learn that they didn't. They actually followed me.

Before Jesus was at the center of it all, the only meaning to my life was happiness, and there was some great yearning in my core that I had no way to satisfy. During that time, I had little to no self-esteem and barely knew who I was. I looked to relationships, drugs, and alcohol to fill that void, yet no matter how much I tried they could not satisfy it. I sought fulfillment in material things and thought the more I bought the happier I would be. I found myself deeper in debt and in that void. I ignored the pain I felt, and if it was too much I would numb it with denial and a night out. While I had many friends, I often felt alone. It was like I was screaming for help with my hand covering my mouth. I was trapped in the darkness I created and didn't know how to get out of it. I didn't realize I needed to be rescued until, after a night of hard partying, Jesus came for me, grabbed my heart, and pulled me out of the darkness.

Meeting Jesus was like coming home, and life in community has been like that too. But in that journey home there have been so many things I have needed to learn. A lifetime of ignoring pain also meant a lifetime of ignoring truth. It is amazing to me that I lived life for so long not knowing—truly knowing—who I was. Just thinking about it makes me sad, but since this discovery I know that there's hope for a person like me. What has been difficult and quite painful at times is when my friends hold a mirror in front of me and I'm too stubborn to take a look at myself. The truth about me seems too unbearable to accept. Rather, I create a better me and choose to accept that person. Therefore, when my friends attempt to show me truth I make it an arduous process. Community not only brings me to the truth but also takes me out of deception and into a place of healing where I have to see the extent of my sinfulness and accept it, especially those things that tempt me to hide in shame. It takes guts to live in community especially when we say that Jesus is the center. Because of this, honesty is a value we try to live out in our own lives and with each other. While it can be painful in the moment, I know that each time my community confronts sin in me it is out of love and their commitment to following Jesus.

My community really knows me. At times they know me better than I know myself, and I am okay with that. One thing they confronted in me was the significance I placed on my feelings and how they affected my perspective. I tend to endure difficult times with optimism and keep myself busy and distracted so I don't feel bad about myself. Sadly, I find myself not able to make decisions because I really don't know what I truly want so I say yes to too many things. In the end, it is just because it all sounds fun. It is easier for me to go with my gut reaction rather than to think through the complexities of a decision. I have found myself in dilemmas where I have said yes to multiple things when I could commit to being in only one place at a time. Living in community has pushed me to be considerate of others and has enabled me to communicate what I really want and what I can and cannot do. I have learned that wanting to (and saying I will) do everything means breaking promises and not keeping my word. It has been painful to accept that I hurt those I love simply because I could not say no at times. I want to be a person of my word, and each time I resort to double booking my integrity is tarnished. Community has been that unyielding support I needed to really change this in me. They have been true friends.

I find authentic friendships to be treasures. I recently heard someone say if the currency of his life were friendships then he is a very rich man. By his definition, I am also a very wealthy person. By simply joining a community, I automatically get lifelong friendships. For the enthusiast, this means more people to enjoy and celebrate life with. Who could ask for more?!

My first experience in intentional community was during college. There were 10 of us in the house, and we hardly knew each other. Regardless, we agreed to keep four commitments while we lived in the house. We committed to invest in our individual growth in Jesus, in each other intentionally in community, to the ministry on campus, and to reach out to our neighborhood. Our relationships grew because these commitments kept us unified in our mission and purpose. I didn't realize how drastic the move out of my suburban apartment and into the inner city was at the time. It felt right because I knew Jesus was leading me. It was not my idea, and it definitely wasn't an impulse I was trying to follow. I knew as I stepped out and obeyed Jesus he would take care of the rest.

In both that community and in this one, my biological family didn't know what was happening or understand our approach to life. I know they've looked at my community and wondered why and how nonrelated people could live like this. Now I am able to better understand their feelings during these transitions in my life. For them, these changes were very strange, and while I love my family deeply, the love and support I receive in community surpasses what I get from them. It's a different kind of love. My community has invested a lot of time and energy in me. They inspire me to be better and keep me accountable to the life I've chosen in Jesus. They have given countless hours to working through the complexities of my life and showering me with support when I felt discouraged or hopeless.

I was carried on the shoulders of my community when my sister, Cassie, died. I wish I could say this came as a shock to us, but it didn't. While Cassie presented herself as a happy-go-lucky person with a bubbly personality, she had a lot of pain that none of us could reach. She isolated herself to deal with her pain, and like me she often numbed her pain with partying and drugs. My four sisters and I loved being silly together, and it didn't take long for us to start laughing and cracking up when we were together. I missed my sister a lot. This was a really difficult time for me. I had a hard time staying focused on work and wrestled with God at night wondering why this happened. Why would he allow something so horrible to happen to my family? What I didn't realize at the time was just how close Jesus was. He was there with us, but more surprisingly he was at the center of my pain. I knew that as I grieved and mourned Cassie's death Jesus was there weeping right beside me. His heart also broke. My family struggled to navigate through this time. We were all total wrecks and often reacted in anger as we tried to get through it all.

In community, there is a mutual understanding that is simple: we are there for each other. Sometimes it's hard for me to ask for help. I think I would rather go on acting like I'm okay and hope that someone notices me before I ask for help. Community fulfills that desire for intimacy in my life. I don't have to expect my family to fulfill this. I am actually free to love them unconditionally with no expectations. I can give to them and love them freely from a place of choice rather than obligation. My family has been through a lot of pain, and I believe we are still dealing with the sudden loss of Cassie. As I pray for my family I know there are many challenges ahead for us. I am confident that Jesus will lead me to make bold statements with the hope that I'd speak from a place of love and sacrifice that I see displayed in community. Because of Jesus, we are recipients of grace, love, and mercy; therefore we are able to give these to each other and can be an example to those who do not know him.

For me living in community has been a tremendous gift, one that I could never repay. As I look at all the friendships I've gained and all of the experiences, from ordinary to profound, I know I've experienced it with people who choose to really know and love me. They know me and celebrate with me, and at times they celebrate because of me. Community enables us to speak from a place of strength. Sometimes a hard word communicates a painful truth when it's needed or gentle words to shower someone with affirmation. For me, this came when someone called me beautiful and intelligent. Living in community uproots your flaws and exposes your brokenness. Yes, it can be painful, but it can also be so good too. Honestly, it wasn't until someone in my community spoke these words to me that I discovered I didn't feel worthy to be complimented in such a way. Like many women, I believed that I didn't deserve to be called beautiful or intelligent. I can now accept that I am a beautiful and intelligent woman. Thanks to my community, I have learned to love myself.

Community as Rescue

My last semester of college, I was exposed and needed my community to come to my rescue. I had finally decided on my classes, and when it was time to schedule them I nearly lost my breath when I found out I couldn't register for my classes because a debt collector pursued me and froze my financial aid. They were collecting $4,000, and paying it was the only way I could register for classes. I didn't have that kind of money, and no way did I have that kind of credit, but Brian did. He helped me by extending his credit to me. This was such a redeeming process for me. I didn't have to act like I had it together, and more importantly I embraced my problem in the company of a trusted friend. Brian not only cleared my name but also restored my dignity by arranging a payment plan so I could pay him back. Brian's commitment to community, and to me, enabled me to graduate. It was quite an accomplishment because I was the first person in my immediate family to do so.

The more I allow my community to speak into all areas of my life, especially during the hard times, the more I get to see the walls of self-deception collapsing in me. Allowing people you trust to love, care for, and protect you can take guts, but it is all worth it. In community, admitting that you have needs and then asking for them is seen as strength. Everyone is needy at different times in community.

In my experience, communal living is the closest to kingdom living. It is in us to put each other's needs before our own. In our home, we try to love each other as we love ourselves so it's normal to shower each other with kindness and affirmation or to serve them by making them a special meal. As we worship Jesus and pursue his heart for the world, along the way I believe that we create real, true happiness to experience together. In the same way my friends restored beauty in my identity, I can pursue others with love in hopes of restoring anything broken in their image as children of God.

I work with vulnerable women, and each time I tell a woman that she is beautiful something inside of our identities as women of God is strengthened at the same time. As a result, the bond between us as women is restored. Ministry to women has been a special call on my life for the past few years. Before I started walking with Jesus, my image of womanhood was broken and befriending women was intimidating and sometimes hurtful. I knew without Jesus, women would continue to view each other as competition rather than sisters. Now that I have Jesus, I can pursue women with love and friendship.

Community as Inspiration

This call for my life came as our community was living in the Philippines serving local ministries among the poor and also women caught in prostitution in metro Manila. This experience opened the eyes of my heart to the darkness of the sex industry that was consuming many women and young children's lives. I would weep some nights after returning home from street outreach with Samaritana, after watching teenage girls be solicited by grown men. I couldn't sleep. I wrestled with the reality that, rather than having a slumber party at their house, these girls were spending hours in the night selling their bodies because their families needed food. Justice for these girls and the many mothers, daughters, and sisters I saw in Manila began to burn inside of me. I knew I couldn't return home the same person I was when we left. After experiencing the heart of God for the least and the lost during our time in the Philippines, I knew I needed to take all of this in—especially the pain I saw on the streets. It needed to scar my soul so that I would never be the same, so that pain would be something that kept me close to Jesus rather than isolated in my euphoric world.

I knew I had to do something in response to all that I experienced there; doing nothing was not an option for me. This meant diving into a mission that would put me in the center of utter pain and tragedy. This meant walking into the pain of others and staying committed until restoration happened. I knew I experienced transformation again because of the direction my life was going. Jesus was leading me to lay my life down for hurting, vulnerable women of my city. In many ways, we were returning home to nothing but God. We had to start all over again. I still remember his gentle voice telling me that he would take care of everything but that I needed to love the women. Of course I was scared when I heard this, but I knew I would not be alone. Together in community the call to pursue and love vulnerable women was affirmed in me. It was blessed, and the ministry Created came to be.

The time we had in Manila was so valuable, but all of my time in intentional community has shaped me like that time. I tell this story because I have seen things I would not have seen if it were not for the collective ambition of our community. And after seeing that pain (which

I would normally turn away from) it is in the strength of community that I have been able to not only see and face that pain but also to actually immerse my life in it. I would not have done that without my community seeing in me that it was possible.

Being the director of Created is the hardest thing I have ever done. It brings out a lot of my insecurities and flaws. At the same time, though, I have never felt as close to Jesus as the way I feel when I am with the women we minister to. Each day I am tempted to operate in my own strength and abilities rather than asking Jesus for help. The pain I see and feel is unbearable at times. As a director, my role causes me to open myself to being hurt, lied to, and betrayed on a regular basis. Why would I want to do this? The enthusiast in me is puzzled and wonders why would I endure pain at all, especially the pain of others. It is because Jesus has transformed my life and my ability to love in the midst of pain. He has redeemed me so I can embrace pain and not run away from it. He has changed my view on brokenness. Now, it is an invitation for us to experience him in a deeper more profound way. This is the message we tell women in Created: that they were created by God for so much more than they have experienced and survived. In hindsight, I think it's poetic irony to think that I would surround myself with other women's pain and be completely happy and fulfilled. Every day, I wonder how it is I do what I do, and then I look around me.

I live in the presence of deeply committed people who live their lives entirely for Jesus and, as a result, inspire me to respond by living the same way. I have eight role models to look to for inspiration and for the love and support I need and really can ask them for it anytime. I see Jesus in them. I experience his presence when we laugh and cry together. All of the experiences I could ever dream of have happened within community. I am a deeply fulfilled person because of community. Instead of giving into the temptation to run, I can face any uncertainty with faith because I have learned to not be afraid of these moments. In community, your pain and struggles are exposed; they are welcomed and nurtured. I have never been abandoned by my community in moments when I am wounded. For me, I feel real growth each time I choose to endure a difficult time because it is done in the presence of my community. I have come to know that life is meant for more than just having a good time and feeling good. Living in community has been an expression of the love I receive from Jesus. It's like my decision to follow and surrender my will to him has led me to community. It has been a journey to finally settling in to the person I was meant to be and to accept the love and support that I have in community. I am grounded in community. Jesus knew that I couldn't continue living the way I was and that I desperately needed help. Living in community has invited me to discover the great love that comes when people are devoted to Jesus and to each other. I am at home in community because I can fully be the person I was meant to be.

11
TYPE EIGHT:
The Challenger
Brian Sanders

The Powerful, Dominating Type:
Self-Confident, Decisive, Willful, and Confrontational

You could say that our community began with the reading of a book sort of like this one. I was a senior in college when I read Tom Sine's energetic and creative book, Live It Up! and I was mesmerized by the idea of simplicity and creativity as grounds for intentional community. College life is pretty communal already, and I was reluctant to move on. I loved my friends, loved the experience of pursuing God with them; for me independence did not need to be synonymous with isolation. I was ready to graduate. I was newly married, and our first baby was on the way. But more than any other characteristic of my life, I was captivated by Jesus and his kingdom.

Two years earlier I made my first trip into the developing world, and I had been forever wounded by the experience. I had an insatiable hunger for understanding both the economic and theological connections to what I had seen. That kind of mind-blowing disparity just ate away at me. I needed answers to questions that haunted my preconceived notions about God and about the American dream. I was just beginning to see that there was a very real relationship between the American dream and the nightmare that is global poverty. It was in this state of prophetic unrest that I read Sine's book.

Community as a More Just Way of Life

The seminal idea in the book for me was the idea of shared living space. Sine made what I thought was an elegant argument. We spend so much time and money in the pursuit of a big house, nice car, and the American dream that we don't have any time or money left for relationship or for the kingdom. Relentlessly creative, Sine painted the picture of a community of people who agreed to share certain key things like lawnmowers and tools so that money could be saved and spent on the kingdom. He took it even further and offered a scenario where houses were built in such a way that backyards, play sets, and laundry facilities could be shared. If four families shared one backyard, it would not only be cheaper but also would save each family two hours a week in time. The only real drawback to living in this way, it seemed, was the apparent lack of personal space. In other words, the only drawback was closeness. Obviously, I don't consider that a drawback anymore.

I entered community because of the allure of a more just lifestyle, as a way to use fewer resources and free up more time, energy, and money for the kingdom. But after doing it for 15 years, it is actually the closeness that is the most precious aspect. As an 8 on the enneagram, I am motivated by injustice. Seeing something unfair has always moved me to act. In less mature times I would fight fire with fire, but meeting Jesus not only arrested my temper and that deeply dangerous spirit of retaliation but also gave me new, more powerful weapons to fight with. Eights tend to define themselves by what they are against. Unlike other types, 8s don't mind conflict. We actually prefer it to injustice. I discovered that Jesus carried a judging fire, promising to balance a world that too often sees the strong exploit the weak instead of protecting them. But Jesus' great power was love. He was not afraid of violence, but he chose to break its grip by submitting to it. Jesus breaks the jaw of the enemy with sacrifice and love. He is the strongest, fiercest, person I have ever known, studied, or considered. I love Jesus for so many reasons, but at the top has to be his choice to become weak to save the weak, to empty himself of strength, to shame the strong by becoming weak. He is more than my savior; he is my teacher and my life's longing.

Community and Confrontation

Without Jesus, 8s can be dangerous. Our preoccupation with power is exactly what I find most reprehensible about human behavior, and it is also what is most broken and dark inside of me. But with Jesus, and this cannot be understated, 8s have the opportunity to take power and redistribute it. I have always believed I was supposed to reorder things. A deep and unspoken wrinkle to my calling is to challenge the status quo by redefining what is normal. Even though, in the beginning, I would not have been able to articulate that, I know now that we are not just trying to find a better way to live; we are trying to heal our culture. We stand together, as community, in an act of defiance against a culture that defines us as consumers and not as a family. We share our things and live on less in resistance to a culture that demands we spend all we have on bigger and better toys, to a culture that has idolized personal property. We have conflict but choose always to stay together, in a revolution of love and reconciliation as the community of Jesus upsetting a system that teaches us to walk away from people with whom we disagree. We love, trust, and share, and even that is a revolution in a culture that is increasingly isolated, sarcastic, and cynical. I have never minded the conflict part of community, because as an 8 I believe we have to confront what is wrong in ourselves, each other, and even the world if we want it to change. If anything, I have been guilty of overplaying that hand, not valuing harmony enough (which is always Monica's challenge to me) because real community holds confrontation and harmony in a paradoxical tension.

Community as Joy

What has been perhaps the most important and healing aspect of community for me personally has been to discover that what we do and who we are is not actually a statement, or a prophetic gesture, or a fight at all. It is just friendship. I am sometimes so future oriented, so principled that I am unable to just experience or enjoy the moment, to see the beauty of the thing right before my eyes. Community has taught me that for all the other reasons, for all the money that can be spent on the poor, for all the time we save to use for the kingdom, for all the character we build together as a community, it is really best understood as a place to love and be loved.

Almost contrary to all the things community represents (existing in tension with that theoretical reality) is the existential truth that community is none of those things. When you are in it, it is not a fight against culture. It is not about conflict and character, and it is not about money or time; it is about us. We are not a principle or a model or a revolution. Maybe we can be that to you, but not to ourselves. To us we are simply us. When I am home or with these friends, I am not a leader or a teacher or freedom fighter (or whatever I think I am); I am simply Brian. The deepest, most elusive aspect of community for people who do not live as we do is that loss of pretention, the loss of guile. The most powerful part of actually living in community is being known and loved—not overestimated, not overlooked, not underappreciated, and not put on a pedestal but just being allowed to be who you are.

So much of my life is leadership. I find it difficult to express in words what it has meant to me to be able to go to a place where I do not exist in a hierarchy, where I am neither over nor under the people in the room. Anyone who leads understands that leadership can be excessively lonely. We are isolated by the responsibility, the decisions we have to make, the burden of leadership. For me, community has been a sanctuary. In the final analysis, I am a better leader because I have a place where I am not expected to be anything other than who I am. The real challenge for me in community is giving everyone else the same grace. What I have found most difficult in community has been embracing people when they do not change.

Community and Patient Grace

Living with the same people for more than a decade affords you a profound insight into who they are, and people are not used to that. We are not used to being known that way, but also we are not used to knowing people so well. It can be hard to understand someone so well that you see what you believe is the solution to their problems or even to begin to understand what it is they need to heal or grow, or whatever. The problem is that all of us have stubborn problems.

For all the growth I can point to in myself—for all the ways community has helped me be a better husband, father, and friend—I am sure my community can point to ways I have stubbornly remained unchanged. This can be one of the hardest parts of living in community. Watching everyone grow and change is rewarding and even exhilarating, but in those stubborn areas where we just struggle to grow and change it can be equally excruciating. My deepest challenge has been to stay committed to the person (as they have stayed committed to me) in spite of their inability to grasp or appropriate some particular discipline or truth.

All of us stay somewhat stuck in ways of thinking and acting that are not healthy or right. In most cases, having community in your life to confront them and to help you move toward Jesus is enough to dislodge those practices. But for all of us, there are a couple of areas that, no matter how many times we confront them, don't seem to budge. Maybe it is because I love them that I am so frustrated by it, but maybe it is also because I want to fix things that are broken. I have had to come to the realization that some things require more perseverance than perspective. We cannot just talk people out of some things. I have had to trust that Jesus is working even if I cannot see it. And I have learned that loving people in spite of their reoccurring flaws is the more poignant and personal expression of love. After all, they do it for me.

What, after all, is the alternative? Do we give people a timeline for change? "You have two years to get this thing right. If you can't by then, you are out." I am ashamed to say that the thought has crossed my mind.

But if I were to apply that rigor to our community, we would cease to be a community of grace, and I would probably have to be the first to go.

I do tend to lead our community, and I think it is important to admit that I do not stop being a leader in the context of our community. It is just not an expectation from them. One way to say it is that they do not need me to be anything other than what I am. When I am free to be who I am, I do still lead. My role has been to keep us centered on Jesus and committed to each other. Much like what we hope this book will do for new communities, we all need to be reminded of what matters and to keep our future hope in sight when we are in the weeds and struggle of daily life.

I am also thankful to my community for receiving me for who I am in total. That has meant allowing me to bring my weaknesses and my strengths into the room, for forgiving the one and following the other. I have a pretty amazing wife and a remarkable marriage. And although we have had our struggles, I have never wanted my marriage to end, not even for a moment. I feel the same way about my life in community. There have been hard moments, but I love these people and they love me. Why would I ever want that to end?

12
TYPE NINE:
The Peacemaker
Monica Sanders

The Easygoing, Self-Effacing Type:
Receptive, Reassuring, Agreeable, and Complacent

When Brian got serious about the idea of living in intentional community, I was 24 years old, and we were married with two young children. The idea was to move into a house in the "inner city" of Tampa and invite another married couple to join us. After we talked about it, I was excited and nervous, but I deeply trusted Brian and his leadership of our family. So I agreed. This idea was new but not totally unknown to me. I am the second of five children and grew up in a Latino home where there were always plenty of people and activity. We also lived with Brian's family for a few years after we graduated from college. However, there is a difference between living with family and deciding to live with lots of people you aren't related to. With family, there is an understanding that no matter what happens you will always love each other and be part of one another's lives. But we were moving into an unfamiliar place with friends we did not know that well, and that made me very nervous. Katy and Jason were brave to join us in this adventure. We knew them from college but were not close friends, and we risked our comfort when we agreed to live together. Our community grew over the years as more people moved in, and now I look back over our years spent living this way and enjoy seeing the ways I've been challenged and the gift it has been in my life.

Living in community brought out many things I knew about myself and other things I didn't know. One thing I knew about myself was that I did not like conflict, and one of the most difficult things about community was facing conflict with others. I am a much more content person when there is peace among people. I grew up in a home where everyone focused on the joy in life and not the pain. It was really difficult in my family to bring up something deep or serious. It was definitely not a part of our family culture. My world changed when I met Brian. He was a deeply passionate, self-confident man who lived life completely devoted to Jesus, and he was a person who was not afraid of conflict. When Brian and I dated, we had our share of conflict. I didn't like it because it made me uncomfortable, but I also had the idea that if you loved someone, conflicts would not be a part of the relationship.

Community and True Peace

In my ideal world, everyone overlooked offenses and lived at peace with one another. However, Brian had a different perspective. He always valued truth over comfort, and he believed if you really love someone you were willing to be honest even if it was initially uncomfortable because it was the only way to understand one another and come to resolution. I avoided conflict because of fear. I was afraid conflict meant risking the harmony. When there was a disagreement, I could confront it or let it go, and I always chose to let it go. I believed that if people disagreed with each other it might lead to unresolved anger that could cause us to be hurt and estranged. Through my marriage and our community, I learned that with practice I could improve at having conflict, and eventually I appreciated it because it could strengthen friendships.

Although conflict is uncomfortable and painful for me, it is better to face it in a relationship where everyone is committed to one another and desiring to understand the other person better. As a peacemaker, it is healing to see this process occur between friends who strive to be loving and truthful at the same time. Peace that comes through honest conflict, I have learned, is better than false peace preserved in hiding how we really feel. Now, I'm able to see the value of facing conflict with someone and loving them enough to work it out. It doesn't really matter if the topic is minor, like where to leave the dish rack, or major, like whether we should continue to live together. In the end, the result is that we walk away understanding one another better and loving each other more sincerely. Conflict exposes us for the darkest parts of our heart and reveals how desperately we need love and forgiveness. The ability to give and receive grace is a great gift. There is a deep security in knowing you are loved and accepted in spite of yourself.

I expected this in my marriage, but I wasn't sure if this would be true in our intentional community too. But we have risked being open and honest with each other with the unspoken truth that we are committed to one another's best interests, and we have developed some strong friendships that have stood the test of time. I never predicted God would use living with five women and two men who were not my relatives to help me overcome my fear of conflict and actually grow by understanding what it meant to have real harmony, true peace, with people I love.

Community as Celebration

There are so many great things about living in community. I love having lots of people around and having a home full of life and activity. I love sharing my life with friends who love me and accept me for who I am. Part of my Latina culture is having lots of people around to celebrate and enjoy life with. I love making way too much food and seeing many mouths devour it. Nothing compares to a house full of laughter and joy. Living this way allows me to have not only my immediate family around but also plenty of others to share life with.

When our children were younger, Brian traveled a lot because of his job, and many times someone might say how sorry they were that I was home by myself. I wasn't quite sure how to respond since I did not feel lonely or sad. I missed Brian, but he was the one leaving all the action to be alone. I was thankful there were always helping hands close by, friends to share a meal with, and someone to talk to. These were priceless gifts I know many young mothers wish they had. There are also practical gifts like having to cook dinner or wash dishes only once or twice a week, and every time I had a baby (we have six children now) there were many friends around to celebrate with me and help me in whatever way I needed. It meant so much to me. One friend who is very artistic and creative celebrated with us by decorating the house when we came home from the hospital with little signs everywhere including up the stairs leading to my room. When I opened my door there was a basketful of snacks and goodies next to a rocking chair. I felt so much love, and I was so happy I had others to share my joy with.

A value I learned from my parents is that life is all about sharing with those you love. It is what matters most in the end. It was never a spoken value, but I experienced it any time I was around them. Living in community is a reflection of this value. My kids know they are loved not only by Brian and me but also by these five "aunties" and two "uncles." They know if they need anything they can ask them, and they would not hesitate to help. These wonderful friends are the best role models I could ask for. If my kids could grow up and have the depth of character and love our community has I would be very happy. I know I would not be the woman I am today if I did not share this friendship with them. Each of them sees the worst in me and still chooses to be my friend and love me through it. There are times when

I am very judgmental. I know how ugly it is, but I struggle with it. In those times, I am still forgiven and accepted. Sometimes I struggle to be patient with my kids, and often someone in my house can sense this frustration and asks if they can help by giving me a break or lending a hand. It is a reminder to love my children.

There is a deep bond in sharing joy, but maybe an even deeper one in sharing sorrow. We have shared the death of loved ones, accidents, difficult times in life, and trouble with our kids, jobs, or marriages. This has been challenging but healing as well. In difficult times, I want to keep things to myself because of my pride and also because of how uncomfortable it makes me. Sorrow disrupts peace. I have seen my friends be trustworthy and loving all these years, and it has become easier to share my sorrows with them. In a time when my marriage or my parenting was struggling, these are the women I turned to when I was undone and thought I was going to lose my mind. They comforted me, prayed for me, and listened to me. I trusted these friends with everything dearest to my heart. This is just another way God has reminded me that he is good and that he provides for his children. I was reminded that he did not forget about me. He loved me, and he was trustworthy.

Community as the Face of Jesus

Jesus uses community to help me understand him better. He says, if someone asks you for forgiveness over and over, forgive them. This is easier said than done, but with his help it is possible. We have a lot of practice forgiving each other, but we are also recipients of this amazing gift. Jesus also teaches us to love our neighbor as ourselves. Community brings out things that are already in our hearts, like selfishness. It is a constant struggle, but we get to practice overcoming it daily. Jesus teaches us to depend on our creator for everything and to carry one another's burdens. There are many nights we sit around sharing a problem in our lives that seems impossible to solve. As a community, we are able to share a different perspective or wisdom or to just listen. It is also an opportunity to go to God together in prayer and remember again how much we need him. The longing of our heart is to know Jesus more and to be like him. I think he uses us in each other's lives to do that. I believe it could happen in other ways, but by overlapping our lives we have made an intentional decision to love one another and all that includes.

My community allows to me to realize how needy I am. In moments of realizing my neediness, there is God's grace for all around me with kind words from an accepting friend. When I see Jason, Katy, Jeremy, Jessica, Crystal, Jennifer, and Joann living a life totally for Jesus it makes me want to join them by doing that too. When I see Jennifer come home from someone's house where she cares for them as a hospice nurse and shares her heavy heart because she sees the pain the family is going through, she is filled with compassion. I see Jesus in her, and I want to be more like him. When I talk to Katy and hear about her visit with her sisters and how she cares for them as a mother should because she has a pastoral heart for them, I see how she has been proactive to help rescue a sister from a bad life situation, and I see Jesus. When I hear of all the blood, sweat, and tears Jeremy gives to see students on campus encounter Jesus in a real way they can relate to, I see Jesus. When I hear of Crystal speak of leading, serving, and loving her artistic friends who need God and her perseverance when it is hard, I see Jesus at work. When Jason shares his heart and passion with many forgotten men who meet in his home and shares hope with them as he walks with them in their struggle to live a life free from addiction, I see Jesus. When Jessica does not call attention to herself yet is always serving someone and being willing to help no matter how big or small the task and rarely complaining, I see Jesus again. As Joann spends her days pouring out her energy, attention, and love on women who have experienced such pain, she often cries when talking about and continues to serve them out of love day after day; I see Jesus in this. Brian is another amazing person, but maybe I am biased. He is a leader among leaders who empowers others to dream big dreams for God and then helps them actually carry them out.

I want to be more like Jesus when I look around me and see these beautiful servants, and maybe that is the best argument I can make for community. I am infinitely rich, and even with all of its challenges I would choose to do it all over again.

PART III
practice

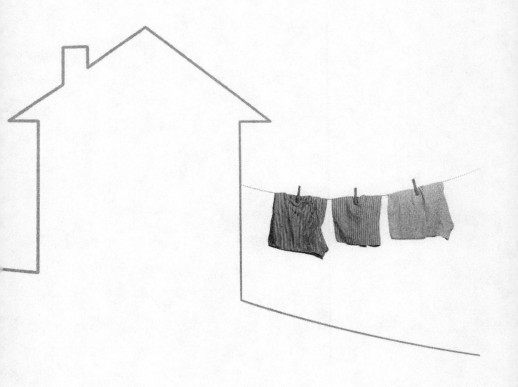

13
Fishing Together:
Community as Mission

It is hard to know exactly what the disciples believed they were saying yes to when they made the decision to follow Jesus. Sure, there were cultural expectations for becoming a follower of a traveling rabbi. They no doubt assumed they were going to travel with him, learn stuff, maybe even get closer to God. Maybe they also knew that community was a part of the invitation. To walk with the same people under the guidance of the same teacher, to bond through trials and travel, can be a powerful communal experience. Yet as we examine the spectrum of life-rocking events they would encounter, it is hard to believe they did not all at some point look at each other shaking their head and ask, "What have we gotten ourselves into?" Jesus knew. He was inviting them into a new family. It must have given the disciples goose bumps when Jesus told his own mother and brothers that these men were his real family (Luke 8:19-21).

Time has given us the space to consider all that Jesus was offering them in community with him. The four core practices I see in that first Christian community are still what I think it will take for us to develop beautiful and lasting community with each other. The first was a relationship with him. His oneness with the father notwithstanding, the disciples got an intimacy with God that no people had ever known. What would become commonplace for the generations of spirit-filled disciples who would succeed them was that they were able to watch Jesus be God on Earth. What a sight to see. We know that the sight often produced awe and worship.

1. Worship

This is the first aspect of biblical community. It is the worship of the triune God revealed by Jesus. If communities are to last, it will be because they are centered first on their personal relationship with God. Christian community is built on the foundation of a collective vertical relationship with God. Paul's definition of worship was surrendering our whole lives to him (Romans 12:1). That is certainly consistent with the call of Jesus on his followers. It was, and still is, to lay down our nets, sell all we have, and follow him. Jesus asks for everything when he invited a person into his family. It is a trading in of one way for another. This is biblical worship. Communities are strongest when they are in agreement about what Paul called "the surpassing worth of knowing Christ Jesus our Lord" (Philippians 3:8). Trying to build lasting community with people who disagree on this fundamental metaphysical reality will cause that group to struggle to build community, and they will never experience koinonia.

2. Self-Reflection

The second aspect of the call of Jesus, which is connected to the first, is a deeper understanding of ourselves. The disciples may have been happy with their simple worldview; work, look after your family, do good, try to please God. But Jesus invites them into the deepest questions the human heart can bear to ask. He took them on a journey of complex ethics, the supernatural, Trinitarian theology, destiny, and human depravity. Listening to him must have generated an almost daily crisis of faith and self-understanding in the disciples.

I think healthy community is made up of reflective, thoughtful, and introspective individuals. It may seem counterintuitive, but the best community members are those who spend enough time alone. Think of a compass (Figure 1). The vertical line pointing north and south could represent the importance of both a worship relationship with the Father (transcendent and triune). The same line pointing south could be considered the internal life a disciple, still related to worship; we look inward as we look upward. True worship should produce awe of God and then self-reflection. Standing in the presence of God has always produced a kind of awkward self-awareness; it is part repentance and part accounting. In other words, it is seeing who God is (in some limited aspect) and then demanding an answer from ourselves, who am I then?

Isaiah is a good example. His encounter with God ends in his realization, "Woe to me, I am a ruining, I am a man of unclean lips" (Isaiah 6:5). It is as if seeing God for ourselves exposes us for what we are not, and an accounting is demanded. This is my simple caution to pure extroverts: You may think that living in intentional community would be a dream come true (people around all the time), but if we do not nurture the private internal life, we will struggle to enjoy the public external life of community.

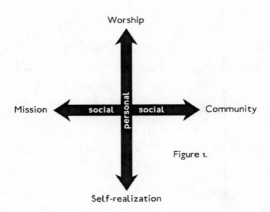

Figure 1.

3. Community

If the vertical pole of the compass represents the value of personal/individualized components of community, imagine similarly a horizontal line that represents the social components. On one side we have our relationships with each other—relationships bonded by the commitment to Jesus. We can call that community. This is most obvious of the four components since we all understand that building community with each other is really possible only when we are with each other. This book is largely about the component on the east of our compass, so I will not belabor the point here. However, it should be said that healthy community will depend on meaningful time spent with your housemates. There is no substitute for time and space to talk, listen, and care for each other. Even though in our community we try to eat together every night, we are rarely all at the dinner table at the same time. So we have made it a habit to set aside Wednesday nights to all be present at dinner. Every Sunday night, we have been meeting in our living room for more than a dozen years, with no agenda—just to be together, to laugh, to cry, and to get off our chests whatever is weighing us down. Sharing space is not the same as sharing life, and time is the core commodity of life.

4. Mission

The other side of the horizontal pole, which requires the most intention since it is the most neglected and the least obvious, is mission. One side is about strong relationship with the people of God; the other side is about a focus on people who are far from God. Most communities do not understand just how important an external focus is to the health and sustainability of an intentional community. Let's consider the alternative.

Let's say a community forms with the dream of absolute belonging, a family that will always be there for each other. But they are sinners, and they bring their struggles and their dysfunction into the house and into their relationships. Given enough time, those dysfunctions cause tension and then conflict, and then the energy of the group turns to fixing those problems. The members become so concerned about the problems in the group that it begins to monopolize their thoughts, their prayers, and finally their time. Each night, hours are spent parsing, struggling, succeeding only to fail again, rehashing, and recovering from the same problems over and over again. Stubborn as the problems seem, the group redoubles its efforts, neglecting work, outside relationships, everything, only to spiral down the same trap. There is little or no time for mission or outside investment since the struggles of the group become so all encompassing, until finally an impasse is declared. Defeated and exhausted, the group disbands.

This is not a fictional story. It is a kind of confession from those of us who love intentional community. In the interest of complete honestly, I must confess this happens. More often then I want to admit. As I have witnessed and analyzed these breakdowns in community I always come to the same conclusion: There was not a common mission. No relationship can bear unmediated scrutiny. If we focus all of our zeal for God into the one aspect of community (the east side of the compass) thinking this is how you build real community, we will only discover more and more flaws. No one can survive that kind of scrutiny, and that is not what community was meant to be. Certainly, iron sharpens iron, and as we live together we will see, confront, and grow. But if that is all we spend our time doing we will not survive. The truth is we need to trust Jesus to lead and grow his people. Sanctification is the work of the Holy Spirit, and while he often uses community to do that work it is not our responsibility to fix, improve, or otherwise alter the people in our community.

The biggest lesson I have learned in 18 years of being married to Monica is that it is not my job to change her. Once I made peace with that truth, that she belongs to Jesus and that it is his work inside her that will see her grow and change, our marriage has been so much healthier. I have always loved her, but I also saw flaws in her that I thought she should really change. I thought I was helping her by trying to effect that change for her. Honestly, though, I wanted her to change because those things bothered me. Deciding to love Monica exactly as she is, saying and meaning that if she never changed I would love her just as much, has liberated me. Likewise, in community we need to be ready and available to God to work on something with a person but then to release that to God as we are busy with the work of mission.

I have always been inspired by Paul's heart expressed in Romans 16. In spite of the strategic importance of a city like Rome, he argues that they really don't need him. He says, "…You are competent to teach each other, full of the Holy Spirit but I am called to the Gentiles." His heart is the heart of balanced community: "I love you; I want to be with you, if I can come through Rome and be with you I will. But I have to prioritize Spain. You have the Holy Spirit to instruct you; you have each other, but they have no one. They have not even heard the good news about Jesus."

In the same way, mission should define the priority of community. Being with each other should be like shelter from the trials and strain of life in mission. As I argued in Chapter 3, people are made for conflict. We all have inside of us a sense of justice, and to one degree or another we have to figure out what it is we are against, what it is we are fighting. When we are not clear on our mission, we look inward and find mission (something to fight against) within the community. That is deadly.

Community is a powerful tool in the hand of God, and we ought to wield it toward the right end. Until Jesus returns, our hearts, hands, and heads have to be focused on his mission in the world. Community is a way to do that better: it is a means to that end. I want to be very clear: I love community, and I believe it is part of what God designed us for. However, he gives us community as a way of accomplishing something that is impossible without it. The church is not the goal; the kingdom of God is the goal. Jesus is building his kingdom, and his church is charged to serve that cause. We are his, and our communities should be his. A part of what it means to rightly appropriate our worship is to preach the gospel, liberate the poor, and usher in the kingdom of God around us. A community that understands that will bond around that common goal. They will be full of grace and not scrutiny for each other. And in the end they will actually accomplish something. All great teams experience a kind of community as they work toward a common goal. Even secular community is possible when there is a common goal and that goal is pursued together. But when we lose sight of our goal we turn inward and become destructive.

In our experience communities do not necessarily have to share the same mission, although that is preferable, as long as there is common mission to Jesus and his cause you can bond over that struggle. Life without mission is dangerous and insular. Community without mission is not worth doing, and in my experience it will not last.

When Jesus called Peter, he asked him to leave everything behind. Although Peter could not know all that was in store for him, Jesus did give him a clue as to what his future would entail. Looking at the life work of Peter to that point and drawing from the day's events, Jesus explained, "Come and follow me. And I will send you out to fish for people" (Matthew 4:19; Mark 1:17). The invitation to follow Jesus is an invitation to do what he does—to make his mission our own. The invitation into his community of disciples was preeminently an invitation to mission, to fishing for people. In the same way that Jesus was fishing for him, he would fish for others. In the same way that Jesus built his community to serve his mission, so should ours be built to serve his mission.

14
Taking Your Time:
Stages of Development

Relationships are complex, beautiful, and infinitely frustrating. Each relationship added means an exponential increase in that complexity. Most of us took a step into community in response to some idealistic impulse. That is, we entered into community because we thought it was the right thing to do. That same impulse can add complexity to what is an already confusing matrix of intent, need, and expectation. We may all come into community because we think it is the right thing to do, but even that sense of righteous action is different for each of us.

I know communities that were formed more out of necessity. Someone needed a place to live, and space was made for them. They are intentional about living together, but it is because it was needed. Once that need is met (and righteousness is satisfied), the same generosity from the host is lost in the practical realities of life together. Others enter into community because they sense a relational shallowness in their lives, hoping that this step toward deeper sharing will produce "real" community with others. The ideal is community itself. Others see the New Testament community as a model not just for church practice but also for lifestyle decisions. And so it is right to live in intentional community. Still others, sick of American consumerism, want to share housing for its fiscal upside, embracing a more just sharing of resources in defiance to a world intoxicated with private property, luxury, and personal wealth. In all cases, we do it because we think we are right to do it. And that is good. But what moves us into the house will not, in the end, be enough to keep us there.

Growing through the Stages of Community

More than a decade with basically the same core group of people has afforded us a unique perspective, not only on what community is but also on how it becomes what it is. What should be clear by now is that community is not a static concept; it is dynamic, and it always defies our attempts to contain or define it. Having said that, I have noticed that most communities go through stages of development. Being able to identify these stages when they are happening actually becomes pretty important if we want to survive (personally and as a community). I want to outline those stages and their transitions so that when they happen you can interpret them with some perspective and can understand that sometimes what looks like a disaster is actually a remaking, a chrysalis of your community into something better.

Stage One: IDEALIZATION

Most communities begin in optimism. It may be guarded, but we enter into the prospect because we nurture the hope that God will reward our faithfulness and pursuit of biblical community with instant intimacy. In many cases that is exactly what we seem to experience. It is especially true in cases where the people who are living together have a lot in common (e.g., ethnicity, socioeconomic status, gender). Monolithic communities tend to start well. It is what we hoped it would be: fun. In this stage we tend to press in to the perceived advantages of community. We are projecting our ideals into the experience. We tend to see what we were looking to see.

If we entered community for the relationships, we really enjoy having people around and being together. If it was more about the economy of community, we really enjoy the efficiency of shared household responsibilities. We see why people do this: it is fun, relational, and efficient. Because we are more positive in this stage we tend to be on our best behavior, so to speak. Some of this stage is real. We are acting out of our idealization (the realization of our best ideas about community), and therefore our behavior is anomalous to our usual patterns. This stage is fueled in part by our improved, value consistent behavior as well as our desire to overlook the failings of others to see our ideal of community realized. In other words, we act nicer than usual, and we are more gracious that usual. We will tend to overlook perceived slights or annoyances from our new community because we want it to work, and, after all, we thought it would.

It is kind of like buying an expensive used car. No matter how excruciating the decision is to spend the money and buy the car, once you make the purchase you are committed. Pleased with your decision, you enjoy the extra features of the car more so because you paid so much, and you tend to downplay the flaws in the car (like the price). It is part optimism and part self-fulfilling prophecy. We need the car to be a good deal, so we focus on its positive features and downplay its flaws. And then the car breaks down.

I once bought a van at auction. It was so cheap I couldn't believe it. For some time I reveled in every fancy feature on the van. All the bells and whistles were there, and the best part was that I had paid so little to get it. I was a genius car buyer, and I was content with that self-evaluation. I wanted to keep it that way. When the van started to break down, I wanted to deny the seriousness of the problems. It's still worth it, I told myself. But when I finally admitted that a cracked engine block made the car a real lemon, my whole perception and evaluation of the initial purchase changed. Dramatically.

The ideation stage tends to come crashing in on itself when we see the proverbial crack in our community's engine—some serious flaw that no doubt was there from the beginning but that our idealism made us blind to see. I am not suggesting that we substitute pessimism in place of our idealism or that we just never enter into community because we know that it will be exposed, in some way, as critically flawed. On the contrary, I argue that we should enjoy the idealistic stage for as long as we can. But know that that when it stalls out and some real problems present themselves, you are just like every other community, and it is time to get real.

Stage Two: CONFRONTATION

Every community has to face its own initial false perceptions and expectations. Community begins with our ideals, and that is surpassingly good because it causes us to take a step toward something extraordinary. However, the same ideals that moved us into community can become an obstacle to the community's development. When the way we thought it was "supposed to" be is different from the way it actually is, we have come to the edge of the confrontation stage. Since the idealization stage is so great, many communities fight to stay there. Denial is the primary tool of the late stage one community. Some might see the problems before others, and still others might agree with the newly exposed challenges but simply not want to address them. Remember, addressing these problems doesn't just mean the introduction of conflict into the idealistic environment it means the end of it. Confrontation will mean real, face-to-face, eye-to-eye acknowledgment of sin and sacrifice. It is hard. However, I have not seen a community that was able to progress without it. Fighting it will make it only more painful when it does (and it inevitably will) occur. It does not always involve sin, but it does always involve sinners. Sometimes we want to pull God into our conflict (usually to side with us), but the truth is that some of the most challenging dynamics are not a matter of sin.

There is a saying that people who live in community are fond of: Everybody wants community, but nobody wants to do the dishes. Is it a sin to forget to do your dishes? No more than it is a sin to get angry when they don't get done. But we have to be real about how that lapse makes us feel and how the consistent neglect of small things conspires inside us to kill love. It seems to me that real love (God's love) is not possible in the first stage. That idealism is more about personal fulfillment. Even if I offer hospitality to someone, which is seemingly an act of sacrifice, I am really just fulfilling my own self-image as a generous hospitable person. It is not until we face the pain of offering hospitality to a sinner, who is at times inconsiderate and who has different values from my own, that I find out whether I am actually capable of love. I call this stage confrontation because it is filled with conformation, on multiple levels.

First, there is the confrontation of the expectations and ideals we had going in to community. Second, it involves a confrontation of the people in community who are upsetting our sense of home. Third, it means the confrontation of our own sinfulness as we discover we are not as gracious, flexible, or selfless as we thought. Just confronting the one without the others will lead to despair. Confrontation in itself is not love, but it is a necessary condition in which love is possible. A relationship that will not confront cannot love. Likewise, a community that will not confront cannot love.

In the same way that the idealization stage stubbornly focuses on the positive, so the confrontation stage focuses on the negative. And in the same way the idealization phase is unhealthy for its lack of realism and balance, so too the confrontation phase tends toward a false negative view. Sometimes the degree to which a community has resisted the confrontation stage, they will linger there. A blowup can then entrench the community in a place of negative (and false) assessment of itself. In the same way that the idealization stage nurtures the notion "we are right," the confrontation stage can nurture the notion "we are wrong."

That realization of brokenness offers the first real threat to the sustainability of the community. People will inevitably want to give up at this point. But don't. You are close to something special. Pressing through and recommitting to the original goals is crucial at this point.

In fact, remembering the idealism of the first stage while in the throes of the second leads a community into the third.

Stage Three: REALIZATION

If the second stage is characterized by conflict, the third stage is characterized by growth. Confrontation in itself does not produce growth; it has to be accompanied by renewed commitment and love. When I am confronted by my community and I do not leave, but instead listen, share honestly, and repent, something incredible begins to happen. I grow. The real payoff in community starts to come in the realization stage. It is not that the pain and challenge of confrontation is gone. On the contrary, this next stage is kind of a coalescence of the first two. Realization would be defined as idealistic confrontation. It is the paradoxical truth that we are community because we wrong each other and because we forgive. We need each other.

The pain of the confrontation continues in the realization stage, but the benefits of the growth begin to present themselves. You know a group is in this phase of development when you ask them, "How is it going?" and they all say, "It is hard but good." The paradox that things that are hard can also be good for us and that there is no growth without change and pain is the realization.

This stage is full of hope and full of personal development, and in my mind it is the beginning of the kind of community most of us never experience. I have become convinced that most Americans never experience true community in their lifetimes. We look for it in the nuclear family, only to suffer the setback of divorce or to see that unit relegated to holiday gatherings, which are full of decades of dysfunction and unconfronted weirdness. In the same way that people try to live a life without God by finding idols and alternative systems where they can invest their faith, so people try to live without community (which seems just as invisible) by finding impotent substitutes where they can imagine they belong.

This makes me sad, so in the same way the prophet is called to blow the trumpet to wake a sleeping people, my community feels the call to let Christians know community is real. Until we discover and embrace it, we will not grow and develop into the people God has called us to be. I confess that I do not fully understand the strategy of God to put the gospel and the church into the hands of his people, but I know he has. I see that his intention was to breathe his own spirit into his people, animating them to live and act as his own body in the world—wowing and wooing an on-looking world with power, creativity, and love. We were meant to be the canvas on which God would paint his masterpiece of love and redemption. Shouldn't we know how to live together? And when we do, wouldn't it make sense that our homes would be the most remarkable, the most redemptive? Intentional community is a microcosm of the kingdom of God. It is a place where sinners come, live, and learn to be more like Jesus. It is a place where sin is not ignored or reviled. Like the woman caught in the act of adultery in John 8, we see each other's sin, refuse to condemn, and call each other to a new life without it.

But that is not the end of community. Even one more stage is possible. Communities that are willing to linger in the third stage and to live in the paradoxical tension of true growth can then expect that to mature into something even more extraordinary.

Stage Four: KOINONIA

After we have embraced realized community in the third stage, something beyond that begins to emerge and present itself. As we have already seen, koinonia is the Greek concept enlisted by New Testament writers to describe what they were experiencing in that remarkable moment of history when the Holy Spirit first kissed his church with his presence. It can be translated "fellowship," "communion," and "sharing," but it carries with it a spiritual connotation. More of a pathos, koinonia is something that is hard to describe but something you will know when it happens. It is my personal conviction that all people experience it in a different way—perhaps connected to the place of their greatest longing or what they perceive as their greatest hope. Not that koinonia takes the place of God, because it does not. It is like the grace of God; when we truly experience it, it causes us to glorify God for it because we know something so pure could come only from him.

Koinonia is about being. It is about security; it is feeling that I am deeply flawed, hurtfully selfish, yet strong, potent, and beautiful. It is to expose what we deeply hope and fear about ourselves at the same time only to discover we are accepted as we are. It is to be at home. And it is finding that home to be with people in the presence of God. It is deeply spiritual, yet it does not need any of the trappings of religious activity. It is a condition, not a practice. You know you have touched koinonia when you no longer have to do or say anything as a community—when simply being together is refreshing and provides a shelter from the storm.

Maybe you are a type 6, and you have struggled with fear your whole life; koinonia means when you are with these people you are no longer afraid. Maybe you are a type 2 and you need people to need you to feel significant; koinonia will mean feeling significant for no reason. Maybe, like me, you are an 8 and you are always feeling the ebb and flow of the dynamic of power around you; koinonia means being with a group of people that makes you forget about power altogether. This kind of community is a place where you can let your guard down because there are no threats present, where you can let go of your insatiable desire to succeed, or be different, or be the same, or have everyone like you. It is a place where we are loved in a way that is like the way that God loves us, without condition or demand. In a very real way it is the coming of the kingdom of God.

Jesus once compared the suffering that his people would endure to childbirth.(John 16:21) His intention, I believe, was to encourage them: although the pain would be extreme and that we would long for an end to the agony, not only would an end come, but also the suffering would produce an unspeakable joy. I love the childbirth analogy because it is about people. To feel relief from suffering when it ends is self-evident. To feel some sense of joy or satisfaction from persevering through suffering is less obvious, but still most of us understand that. When we work hard and make it through something, there is some healthy pride in the accomplishment. But the birth of a child is not like that. The birth event (which I have had the privilege to witness six times) is not filled with pride or even relief; it is filled with joy. It is filled with joy because the event is defined not by the end of something or by the perseverance (which was significant). The event is eclipsed by the new little human being who has burst into our world, storming our reality with the joy of her coming. The joy comes with the baby. The kingdom comes like that. It does come through suffering and does require perseverance, but the joy and power of its coming is so real and new that it demands to be the single focus of our joy.

Part of what we are all trying to say is that real community is the coming of the kingdom. Into a lonely, isolated, competitive, and selfish world, the kingdom comes. It comes in us as we suffer through the throes of these transitions. It can be aborted. It can be abandoned. It can be neglected. Just living together is not enough. We have to persist in our belief that the presence of Jesus with his people can usher in the kingdom. But we have to do that as we struggle through the stages that present us with reasons to quit, to find that new life we initially dreamed about is possible, only if we persevere till the end.

15
Questions People Ask Us

There are lots of permutations of intentional community, all with something to learn and teach. We tend to field very similar questions, and as we answer we trust readers to understand that these answers represent our approach and are not an attempt to dogmatize our way over another. Nevertheless, we know that our approach has worked for us and is at the very least a healthy possibility for those looking to start or improve their own intentional community.

Does living in community mean a loss of privacy?

For us it has not meant the loss of privacy. All of us have a sense of public and private space. In some neighborhoods, the whole house including the front and backyard is considered private space. In some neighborhoods, front yards are places where neighbors congregate and talk. Others include their front porch as a kind of public space, leaving the inside as private. When I was in college, our dorms had what we called commons. We all had our own room but there were dining rooms and living areas where we could gather and hang together. This is a lot like our arrangement. We share a kitchen, living room, dining room, front porch, and backyard, but our bedrooms are our private space.

And in our house our rooms are in separate sections of the house. This has worked really well for us. In a decade I can count on one hand the number of times I have gone into one of my housemate's bedrooms. Almost always it was to fix something. We just don't do it. So privacy is actually very important to us, maybe even more important than most people. Our distinction between public and private space is very clear for us. We just never violate it. When one of us is in our room with the door closed, it is like that person is not home at all. We take care not to even knock on each other's doors; when we are in our space we deeply respect that. Maybe because we have less of it, we deeply value privacy.

Isn't this hard on marriages?

It is hard to have a fight in community. It is hard to be a jerk to your spouse or to be angry and hold a grudge. It is very hard to yell when you fight, and it is extremely hard to be abusive or act in a way that would otherwise embarrass yourself. So you tell me, is that good or bad for a marriage? Living in community has made it very hard for me to stay angry with Monica. We can have an argument, but it would have to be a low-volume event in our bedroom. Otherwise, we risk someone else listening in. For us, that has provided a healthy boundary and accountability.

It can be hard to find time to be completely alone. We do have a nice bedroom with a TV and a computer in it, so there is space for us to read, talk, work, or be alone. And we have had to make sure to take time away together regularly (both dates and getaways). It is not that different from having children. Our kids share our house, too, which means we have to learn to give some space a public category and keep our room as a sacred private space for us. In all, I think all of the couples would say that living in community can at times feel cramped, but the benefits far outweigh that loss of private space. Our marriages are stronger because we are accountable for how we treat each other.

I think we all act more Christlike because we know that others are watching in on our lives. We do not go out of our way to comment on each other's marriages; for the most part we give each other space, but when there is a glaring problem we are there to talk through it, often protecting the weaker member in the relational dynamic. For us, marriages are stronger in this context.

What is it like to raise kids in community?

The couples in our community all have subtle differences in the way we raise our kids. Jeremy and Jessica and Jason and Katy homeschool their kids. Monica and Brian do not. Some highly value order and discipline; others put more emphasis on creativity and free thinking. But we all respect each other's calling as the parents of our kids. We all respect that by deferring to each other's parenting style when dealing with someone else's child. It has worked for us.

Having said that, we do influence each other in how we raise our kids. Watching someone do something well is always inspiring and valuable. We tend to emulate the strengths and just ignore the weakness we see in each other. Even so, having other adults in the lives of our kids has helped them to develop love and respect for all adults. Having single women in our community has been invaluable as we have begun the teenage years, as these women reinforce our values and provide cool, Godly examples for our girls to watch. Our kids don't complain because they have never really known anything different.

What is it like to be a kid who grows up in community?
(answered by Eve Sanders)

My name is Eve. I am 12 years old, and ever since I was born I have been blessed to grow up with so many people surrounding me who love and look out for me and my best interest. For me community means that I share not only a house but also my life with many different people. They teach me and guide me through everything. When I suffer they suffer; when I am overwhelmed with joy they stand by my side and are joyful with me. They are my aunts and my uncles. Even though we are not related in blood, we are all part of a family. For me, every time I am sad, I have much more than just one sister to help me get through it. They love me, and I love them back; they teach me some, and I teach them some.

Since I have lived in community since birth, I really didn't have a choice to be part of community, but I am really just glad I have community in my life. I honestly must say I am overwhelmed to know that I am part of a fruitful community—one that trusts in God with everything, their money, their love, and most importantly their lives. I believe that I need examples, role models, to look up to, and community gives me just that. I currently live with my four aunts, my mother, my father, my one sister, and my four brothers and I have something to learn from each of them. I must agree that all communities have their struggles, and we have been through pointless arguments, but in the end they have made us stronger. From my point of view, I love my community. To me, it is like an oversized family, and I think that no matter what happens we all seem to be drawn together toward our same passion, Jesus.

How do you handle money?

In our household, we all run our own finances privately. We know some communities do what is called a common purse, sharing their money together. While we respect that option, we find that to be so labor intensive as to take away from the grace of community. We did live by common purse when we were in the Philippines together, and it was a good experience. However, that worked mostly because we shared the same income while we were there. Here we all make different amounts of money and do not talk about that part of our lives explicitly (unless someone needs help).

Instead, we all chip in money for common things. One person (Katy originally, then Jennifer) would do the grocery shopping, buying staples for the whole house. We share that cost and those groceries. Most of us would also do some of our own private shopping for little things that we want but don't consider staples (something that most everyone would eat). Since a different person cooks each night, the person cooking might also do some shopping for that night, the cost of which is included in our overall monthly grocery bill. We all pay a share of the grocery, electric, water, gas, and cable/Internet bills. We count our kids as .5 person in the calculation of shares (that's horrible isn't it?).

Each adult also chips in $20 a month to our house fund, which we save until it is needed. Usually, Brian pays for most or all of the house repair and house maintenance (which is fair since he is earning the equity). Other things are always needed (e.g., a new microwave, chairs for the patio, exterminator), and that is how the house fund is spent. Whatever approach you choose with money it is important to make sure that everyone agrees and to reevaluate these choices periodically as things change and certainty or perceptions on the justice of a choice will change over time.

How do you handle something like home ownership?

Originally, I (Brian) owned the houses we lived in. There were two side by side. Each person who jumped in was just paying rent. When we outgrew those houses, we found a bigger one that was co-owned (we were both on the note) by the Sanders and the Thompsons, and everyone else paid rent. When Jason and Katy felt called to move into their own house, Brian and Monica bought them out of their share ownership in the house. For a time we also offered the single women the option of paying slightly more rent to buy a percentage ownership of the house. Some did that; others opted out, preferring the lower rent so that they could make other investments with their money.

As the owner of the house, I have always tried to charge the absolute minimum for living there. Over the years we have charged as little as $75 a month and as much as $250, taking into consideration the ability of the person to pay, the number of people living in the house, and the size of the space the person is occupying. As the owner I have always erred on the side of being taken advantage of (as opposed to taking advantage) because I don't want there to be any doubt when money is changing hands that I want to serve and sacrifice for everyone. For people just starting up, I would recommend that you not try to co-own a house out of the gate. It puts extra pressure on the relationships that you don't need. Ideally, you would want the owner of the house to be able to afford the mortgage even if no one were living there or if the people living with you could not pay. Again, this relieves the pressure of having to make community work because of financial demands. Co-ownership is an option (and we have seen it work), but the relationships have to be rich in trust.

What is it like to be single living in community with married people? (answered by Crystal, Joann, and Jennifer)

Living in community as a single person is mostly great even though there are drawbacks. Being single is often lonely, but in community we are surrounded by others. From our perspective, married couples offer consistency and rhythm to the single life. Overall, the benefits for the communal single far outweigh the negatives.

Accountability within community is a gift. We find that we are reminded of our purpose. Each major life transition is greeted with wisdom and prayer from fellow members. Sharing your life in community will mean sharing the details of your life and being vulnerable in front of a group of people, which can be hard if the married people are not also sharing. For both single and married people, there has to be mutual agreement on equal sharing.

In community, married people are not just a couple; they are unique individuals. As single people, this allows us to engage in friendships one on one and also to see healthy marriages up close. We are a part of the family and have a significant role that speaks into the lives around us.

Occasionally there is loneliness for us as single people in community. In our experience, these are felt during special family times, vacations, and couples' night out. These moments are fleeting and for the most part have very little impact on our overall experience.

Every single person will need different things; don't be afraid to ask. We have seen some communities have just one person who is single, and we think that can be isolating and unhealthy. We would recommend that if the community is going to be made up of married and single people there should be at least two singles.

How do you handle chores and household responsibilities?

Each person in the house takes turn washing dishes. Brian handles all the repairs and outside house work (and for that reason does not wash dishes). We keep our own space clean, and Monica, who is home most, tends to clean the rest of the house on a regular basis. Periodically, when Monica needs help (spring cleaning) she will ask for it, and everyone else will chip in. Likewise, every couple of months we have a house workday where we take half a Saturday to work on the house (inside and out) all together. In the past we have set up clear chore duties, but as we have reached a level of comfort with each other we tend to just chip in when it is needed and all carry an attitude of servanthood toward each other and keeping the house clean.

What if someone wants to Leave? How does that work?

All healthy communities need to have both a front door and a back door. There should be a way in, and there should be a way out. Invariably, life brings changes, and if we love each other we will celebrate and support the changes that God is initiating. Everyone is very open to the possibility that God might be calling someone to something else. But for us that is the test. We want decisions like that to be made together. It would constitute a breakdown in community (not insurmountable, but a breakdown nevertheless) if someone just announced to everyone that God was calling them to leave. Instead, there has to be an openness from both sides of the question to explore the possibility. As soon as someone senses that change might be God's plan, they would offer that hunch to everyone; we could all together talk through it and pray along with that persons. Of course, in the end it is their decision, but it would be foolish for that person not offer that important decision to the community to consult on. A strong community will consider it without feeling personally hurt but the possibility, and strong community members will submit their decision to leave to the group, inviting their wisdom, perspective, and blessing. In the end, we are trying to discern if making the move is what God is calling all to do, which means we all need to be open to the possibility and support it if it is best. We have had people move out to another house but stay a part of our weekly community meetings. Twice that was best. Most recently, we all walked together through the decision for Jason and Katy to move their family to Germany, a decision they submitted to the community and the community agreed was right (as sad as it was to see them go). Ultimately, the answer is that people can and should leave, but it should never be in anger or unreconciled conflict. Leaving can and should happen, but it should be in response to God's leading.

What about coed housing; isn't that dangerous? How could I share a house with another woman/man?

This is a very important question. We do not want to give the impression that we are not careful and aware of the sexual dimension to what we are proposing. We all have to balance our extramarital relationships with care and conviction. I have had to be particularly careful as someone who is a spiritual leader in the public eye to make sure that my life and reputation are untouchable and an example to others. But all of us, no matter what our position or calling, need to be honest with ourselves and each other about the very real temptation that close cross-gender relationships can bring.

Even though we share a house together, I am never alone with any of the women who live in our house. Again, I will use public and private space as terms to explain our approach. The key is to have cross-gender relationships in public not in private. We agree that this can be applied to physical and relational space. Physically, Christians should take care not to place themselves in compromising positions or even places that might cause others to question the purity of our intentions. At times it will be inconvenient: I might come home and find only one other woman home; when that happens I have to be willing and disciplined to just go to my room until someone else comes home. Believe it or not, it has not been a big problem for us, and it is something I am glad to do if it keeps our house free from accusation or awkwardness. We are not afraid to be in relationship with each other, and sexuality is not something that should be a barrier to community. However, we are all sinners, and we have to also be honest about our weaknesses.

Before you enter into community, it is important that we all check our own hearts toward each other. I ask new communities to be honest (in same-gender relationships) if there is any attraction to a person in the newly proposed community. If there is, we recommend you do not live with that person. Not everyone needs to be able to live in the same household. If there is that kind of attraction, find someone else.

Starting with that monkey on your back is certainly not insurmountable for God, but it is foolish. Community is hard enough without adding an inappropriate sexual attraction. If you can honestly report that no such attraction exists, then thoughtful, pure relational boundaries coupled with relationships that exist in the open for all to see should protect your community from sexual pitfalls. Honesty, boundaries, and simply living lives in view of one another are enough. All of our relationships, whether same or across gender, are subject to the community. No relationship is off limits to the caring observation of the rest of the community. Codependency, attraction, condescension, and power dynamics are all addressed when they first present themselves so that they are not allowed to mature into full-blown sin. The public nature of our relationships has not made them perfect but has kept them from grievous error. Having said that, we need to be honest with ourselves and the brothers or sisters who keep us accountable sexually; if some kind of attraction or unhealthy connection forms between two people it is important to confess that and to ask the rest of the community how to adjust the relational patterns so that those temptations do not give birth to full-blown sin.

How do I start or find an intentional community?

Finding one to plug into is rare to impossible. Unless it is a part of the culture of your church or you know people well who do it, it will be hard to find one to simply plug into. That is actually the good news, because we need more people to start them. Here are a few simple guidelines for starting an intentional community:

1. **Conceive.** Once the idea is planted in your heart, start sharing that idea with the people in your life. You may be surprised at who responds and who doesn't. Obviously, share the idea with people you like, admire, or otherwise would like to live with. This is not the time or

place for martyrdom. It is not wrong to partner with people you like.

2.   **Explore.** If you have another couple or a few friends who are up for trying it, look around for people who are doing it. Maybe make a field trip to Tampa or somewhere you know people are living in intentional community. Go as a group, explore their practice, ask questions, and begin talking about what that could look like for you.

3.   **Locate.** When people are excited about trying it, look for a place that will fit you. Don't rush into home ownership. If one of you already owns a home that you can use, that is great; that way there is no financial pressure on the relationships. You don't need that. But even this decision should be done together.

4.   **Agree.** First, decide on your common mission. If you come from different churches or have various relational circles, a house church is a great idea. It is something you all can work together on, that can have an emphasis on your neighbors as well as people from your work, school, or families. It can be a great net that once a week you can all create together. In addition to mission, come to agreement on your common values for your house and a general approach to life, meeting, and family. You don't need to figure everything out, but it is good to have agreement on the big things.

5.   **Try.** Enter into a trial period. I think at least a year is a good idea. Make sure that it is clear up front that everyone is just exploring if this is what God wants. There can be no hard feelings if in the end it does not seem to be. Remember this is not for everyone; you are not a failure if you try it out and it is just too difficult for you. Be sure to set a date when you will pray again and have a heart to heart about whether you should continue together.

6.   **Communicate.** Meet regularly to share about your lives and about how living together is going. You have to have protected set aside time and space to be honest and listen to each other. Some communities do very well at sharing their lives with each other during the week; if so you can focus this time more on household business. But others

don't catch up with each other enough during the week, so this time may need to make even more space for just the sharing of your lives (struggles and joys). Communication is so important to community. You have to talk and be honest. Love each other by receiving each other through communication.

7. **Commit.** If the trial goes well and it is "hard but good," then you might want to consider making longer-term kinds of verbal commitments to each other. It does not have to be a time frame; just verbalize your love and commitment to each other. "I am with you guys." "I want to stay here with you guys." The experimental stage is healthy for a while, but if the community always feels experimental (like people might leave at any time) it can begin to erode confidence and create insecurity.

8. **Thrive.** You take it from here. Let the community breath, with people coming in and out, and let it define itself. God will lead you from this point on.

CPSIA information can be obtained at www.ICGtesting.com
Printed in the USA
LVOW101745050412

276370LV00002B/5/P